Empowered Parenting: Unlocking Your Full Potential for Raising Great Kids

Barley Nicola

Published by Barley Nicola, 2024.

While every precaution has been taken in the preparation of this book, the publisher assumes no responsibility for errors or omissions, or for damages resulting from the use of the information contained herein.

EMPOWERED PARENTING: UNLOCKING YOUR FULL POTENTIAL FOR RAISING GREAT KIDS

First edition. April 2, 2024.

Copyright © 2024 Barley Nicola.

ISBN: 979-8224036424

Written by Barley Nicola.

Table of Contents

• • • •

- OVERVIEW OF PARENTING

Parenting is a complex and challenging task that involves the nurturing and upbringing of children from infancy to adulthood. It is a lifelong commitment that requires patience, love, and guidance to help children develop into well-adjusted and responsible individuals. Parenting styles can vary greatly depending on cultural, social, and personal factors, but the ultimate goal remains the same - to raise children who are happy, healthy, and capable of leading successful lives.

There are several key components to effective parenting, including providing a safe and nurturing environment, establishing clear expectations and boundaries, and fostering open communication with children. Parents play a crucial role in shaping their children's beliefs, values, and behaviors through their words and actions. By modeling positive behavior, demonstrating empathy and understanding, and teaching important life skills, parents can help their children navigate the challenges of growing up and becoming independent individuals.

One of the most important aspects of parenting is establishing a strong bond with children through consistent love and support. Research has shown that children who have secure attachments with their parents are more likely to develop healthy relationships, exhibit higher self-esteem, and have better emotional regulation skills. Building a strong parent-child relationship requires time, effort, and patience, but the rewards are well worth it in terms of the child's overall well-being and development.

Effective communication is another crucial aspect of parenting that can help parents understand their children's needs and feelings, as well as provide guidance and support. Creating an open and honest dialogue with children encourages them to express themselves, seek help when needed, and build trust in their parents. Listening actively, validating children's emotions, and offering constructive feedback are important communication skills that can help parents navigate the ups and downs of parenting.

In addition to emotional support and communication, parents also play a critical role in providing for their children's physical and material needs. This includes ensuring access to nutritious food, adequate shelter, quality healthcare, and a safe environment to grow and thrive. Parents are responsible for meeting their children's basic needs, as well as providing opportunities for education, socialization, and personal growth.

Parenting also involves setting boundaries and enforcing rules to help children learn appropriate behavior and develop self-discipline. Consistent discipline and consequences for misbehavior are important for teaching children valuable life lessons and helping them understand the importance of respect, responsibility, and accountability. Disciplinary methods should be fair, age-appropriate, and focused on teaching rather than punishing, to help children learn from their mistakes and make better choices in the future.

Parenting is a dynamic and evolving process that requires parents to adapt to their children's changing needs and developmental stages. As children grow and develop, parents must adjust their parenting style, rules, and expectations to meet the challenges and opportunities of each age and stage. Being flexible, patient, and willing to learn from both successes and failures can help parents navigate the complexities of raising children and building strong family relationships. By providing a safe and nurturing environment, fostering open communication, setting boundaries, and teaching important life skills, parents can help their children grow and thrive. Building strong parent-child relationships, supporting emotional development, and meeting children's physical and material needs are all essential components of effective parenting. By embracing the joys and challenges of parenting with a positive and proactive attitude, parents can help their children reach their full potential and lead fulfilling lives.

- Importance of empowered parenting

Parenting is one of the most important and challenging responsibilities that we face in life. From the moment a child is born, parents are tasked with providing love, guidance, and support to help them navigate the complexities of the world. In recent years, there has been a growing recognition of the importance of empowered parenting in shaping the development and well-being of children. Empowered parenting involves equipping parents with the knowledge, skills, and resources they need to effectively support their children's physical, emotional, and cognitive growth.

One of the key aspects of empowered parenting is the ability to establish a strong and nurturing bond with your child. Research has shown that children who have secure attachments with their parents are more likely to thrive academically, socially, and emotionally. Empowered parents understand the importance of building this attachment early on through responsive and consistent care. By being sensitive to their child's needs and providing a safe and supportive environment, parents can help foster a strong sense of security and trust in their child.

Empowered parenting also involves setting appropriate boundaries and expectations for children. Children thrive when they have clear guidelines and rules to follow, as this provides them with a sense of structure and predictability. However, it is important for parents to strike a balance between being firm and supportive. Empowered parents use positive discipline strategies that focus on teaching and guiding their children rather than resorting to punishment. By setting clear expectations and consequences, parents can help their children develop self-discipline and responsibility.

It is also important for empowered parents to prioritize their own well-being. Parenting can be a demanding and exhausting job, and it is easy for parents to neglect their own needs in favor of their children's. However, research has shown that parents who take care of themselves are better able to care for their children. Empowered parents prioritize self-care activities such as exercise, hobbies, and social connections to recharge their energy and maintain their mental health. By taking care of themselves, parents can model healthy behaviors for their children and create a positive and nurturing environment for the whole family.

Another important aspect of empowered parenting is fostering a growth mindset in children. A growth mindset is the belief that abilities and intelligence can be developed through effort and perseverance. Empowered parents encourage their children to embrace challenges and view failures as opportunities for learning and growth. By praising their children's efforts and progress rather than focusing solely on outcomes, parents can help instill a sense of resilience and perseverance in their children. This mindset is essential for success in school, work, and life, and empowered parents play a crucial role in nurturing it. By establishing strong relationships with their children, setting clear boundaries and expectations, prioritizing self-care, and fostering a growth mindset, parents can create a positive and nurturing environment that supports their children's growth and success. Empowered parents understand that parenting is a lifelong journey that requires patience, dedication, and continual learning. By embracing these principles, parents can empower themselves and their children to thrive and reach their full potential.

- Setting goals for raising great kids

Setting goals for raising great kids is a crucial aspect of parenting that requires careful consideration and planning. As parents, it is our responsibility to guide and nurture our children in such a way that they become well-rounded individuals who are equipped to face the challenges of life with confidence and resilience. By setting clear and meaningful goals for our children, we provide them with a roadmap for success and help them develop the skills and qualities that will serve them well throughout their lives.

One of the key goals that parents should strive to achieve is to instill in their children a strong sense of values and ethics. By teaching our children the importance of honesty, integrity, compassion, and respect for others, we help them develop a moral compass that will guide them in their interactions with the world. Encouraging empathy and kindness in our children can help them become more understanding and compassionate individuals who are able to navigate complex social situations with grace and maturity.

Another important goal for raising great kids is to foster a love of learning and a growth mindset. By encouraging our children to be curious, resilient, and open-minded, we can help them develop a thirst for knowledge and a passion for personal growth and development. Providing our children with opportunities for exploration, discovery, and self-expression can help them develop critical thinking skills, creativity, and a lifelong love of learning that will serve them well in school and beyond.

Setting goals for raising great kids also involves helping our children develop essential life skills such as communication, problem-solving, and decision-making. By teaching our children how to effectively communicate their thoughts and feelings, collaborate with others, and resolve conflicts peacefully, we empower them to build strong relationships and handle challenges with confidence and maturity. Encouraging our children to take initiative, set goals, and make informed decisions can help them develop a sense of autonomy and self-reliance that will serve them well in their personal and professional lives.

In addition to these goals, parents should also strive to help their children develop a strong sense of self-esteem and resilience. By providing our children with love, support, and encouragement, we can help them build a positive self-image and a strong sense of self-worth that will enable them to navigate life's ups and downs with confidence and resilience. Teaching our children how to cope with failure, setbacks, and disappointments in a healthy and constructive way can help them develop grit, perseverance, and emotional intelligence that will serve them well in overcoming obstacles and achieving their goals.

Ultimately, setting goals for raising great kids requires a thoughtful and intentional approach that takes into account the unique needs, strengths, and interests of each child. By tailoring our parenting strategies to meet the individual needs of our children, we can help them develop the skills, qualities, and values that will enable them to thrive and succeed in life. By setting meaningful goals and working towards them with dedication and commitment, we can help our children become the best version of themselves and make a positive impact on the world around them.

Chapter 2: Understanding Child Development

. . . .

- STAGES OF CHILD DEVELOPMENT

Child development refers to the process through which children grow and mature physically, emotionally, cognitively, and socially. Understanding the stages of child development is essential for parents, educators, and healthcare professionals to provide appropriate support and guidance to children as they navigate through different milestones and challenges. There are several broadly recognized stages of child development, each with its own set of characteristics and milestones. These stages include infancy, early childhood, middle childhood, and adolescence. Let's explore each of these stages in more detail to gain a better understanding of the intricacies of child development.

The infancy stage typically spans from birth to around 18 months of age. During this time, infants undergo rapid physical growth and development as they learn to control their bodies and interact with the world around them. Infants begin to develop basic motor skills such as grasping objects, rolling over, and eventually crawling and walking. They also start to explore their environment through their senses, learning to recognize and respond to familiar faces and sounds. Additionally, infants begin to develop emotional bonds with their caregivers, forming secure attachments that are crucial for their social and emotional development in later years.

As infants transition into the early childhood stage, which typically encompasses ages 2 to 6, they continue to make significant strides in their physical, cognitive, and social development. This period is often referred to as the "preschool years," as children in this age group may start attending early childhood education programs or preschools. During this stage, children further refine their motor skills, language abilities, and social interactions. They begin to engage in pretend play, develop a sense of curiosity and independence, and start to understand basic concepts such as numbers, colors, and shapes. Early childhood is a critical time for laying the foundation for future learning and social development, as children start to form relationships with peers and adults outside of their immediate family.

Middle childhood, which typically spans from ages 6 to 12, is a period of significant cognitive and social development for children. At this stage, children become more independent and self-sufficient, taking on new responsibilities and challenges at school and in their communities. They also continue to develop their cognitive abilities, including problem-solving skills, critical thinking, and logical reasoning. Middle childhood is a time when children begin to form a sense of identity and self-esteem, as they navigate through social interactions with peers and develop a better understanding of their own strengths and weaknesses. This stage is also characterized by increased physical coordination and motor skills, as children become more adept at sports and other physical activities.

Adolescence is the final stage of child development, typically occurring from ages 12 to 18. This period is marked by significant physical, emotional, and social changes as children transition into young adulthood. Adolescents experience rapid physical growth and development, with puberty bringing about hormonal changes that impact their bodies and behaviors. This stage is also a time of heightened emotional sensitivity and self-awareness, as adolescents grapple with issues such as identity formation, peer relationships, and future aspirations. Cognitive abilities continue to evolve during adolescence, with adolescents developing more abstract and complex thinking skills, as well as the ability to plan for the future and make decisions based on long-term consequences. It is during this stage that adolescents begin to seek greater autonomy and independence from their parents, while also navigating the challenges and pressures of peer relationships, academics, and societal expectations. From infancy to adolescence, children undergo significant physical, cognitive, emotional, and social changes that shape their personalities and behaviors. By recognizing the characteristics and milestones of each stage of development, adults can better tailor their interactions and resources to meet the needs of children at different points in their journey towards adulthood. Ultimately, a holistic approach to child development that considers the unique strengths, challenges, and potential of each child will help ensure their lifelong success and well-being.

- Recognizing and supporting your child's needs

Recognizing and supporting your child's needs is a crucial aspect of parenting that can have a significant impact on their overall development and well-being. As parents, it is important to understand that every child is unique and has their own individual needs, preferences, and challenges. By taking the time to recognize and support these needs, parents can help their children thrive and reach their full potential.

One of the first steps in recognizing and supporting your child's needs is to pay attention to their behavior, emotions, and communication. Children may not always be able to express their needs verbally, so it is important for parents to observe their child's body language, facial expressions, and actions to better understand what they may be feeling or experiencing. It is also important to create an open and supportive environment where children feel comfortable expressing their thoughts and feelings.

In addition to being observant, it is important for parents to engage in open and honest communication with their children. By talking to your child and actively listening to their concerns, you can gain valuable insights into their needs and preferences. This open dialogue can help parents better understand what their child may be going through and provide the necessary support and guidance.

Furthermore, parents should also consider seeking professional help if they notice any signs of developmental delays, learning difficulties, or behavioral issues in their child. Early intervention can make a significant difference in addressing these challenges and helping children overcome obstacles that may be hindering their growth and development. By working closely with teachers, therapists, and healthcare professionals, parents can find the support and resources needed to help their child succeed.

It is also important for parents to create a nurturing and supportive home environment that promotes positive growth and development. This can include setting clear boundaries, establishing routines, and providing love and encouragement. By creating a safe and secure environment where children feel supported and valued, parents can help their child feel confident and empowered to explore and learn.

Moreover, it is important for parents to prioritize self-care and seek support when needed. Parenting can be a challenging and demanding role, and it is important for parents to take care of themselves in order to effectively support their child's needs. By taking the time to recharge and seek help from friends, family, or professionals, parents can ensure that they are better equipped to meet their child's needs and provide the support and guidance that is necessary for their growth and development. By being observant, communicative, and proactive, parents can create a supportive and nurturing environment that promotes positive growth and development in their children. Through open dialogue, seeking professional help when needed, and prioritizing self-care, parents can effectively meet their child's needs and help them thrive and succeed. By taking these steps, parents can play a crucial role in shaping their child's future and empowering them to reach their full potential.

- Building a strong parent-child relationship

Building a strong parent-child relationship is essential for the emotional, psychological, and social development of a child. Research has shown that children who have a close and supportive relationship with their parents are more likely to thrive academically, socially, and emotionally. Parental involvement and communication play a crucial role in fostering a positive parent-child relationship. It is important for parents to be actively engaged in their child's life, to listen to their thoughts and feelings, and to provide love, support, and guidance.

One of the key factors in building a strong parent-child relationship is communication. Open and honest communication between parents and children is essential for developing trust and understanding. Parents should create a safe and supportive environment in which their children feel comfortable sharing their thoughts and feelings. This can be achieved through active listening, validating their emotions, and offering encouragement and support. Effective communication also involves setting clear expectations and boundaries, and consistently enforcing rules and consequences.

Another important aspect of building a strong parent-child relationship is spending quality time together. Quality time can take many forms, such as playing games, going for walks, doing crafts, or simply talking and bonding. It is important for parents to prioritize spending time with their children, as this helps to strengthen the emotional connection between them. Quality time also provides opportunities for parents to teach their children important values and life skills, such as empathy, resilience, and problem-solving.

In addition to communication and spending quality time together, showing love and affection is also crucial in building a strong parent-child relationship. Parents should express their love and affection for their children regularly, through words, actions, and physical touch. This helps children feel secure, valued, and loved, which in turn boosts their self-esteem and emotional well-being. Love and affection also create a strong bond between parents and children, fostering a sense of connection and belonging.

Moreover, fostering a positive parent-child relationship involves providing support and guidance to children as they navigate the challenges of growing up. Parents should be there to offer help and encouragement, and to teach their children important life skills, such as problem-solving, decision-making, and conflict resolution. By offering support and guidance, parents help their children develop the confidence and resilience needed to thrive in an ever-changing world. Effective communication, spending quality time together, showing love and affection, and providing support and guidance are key elements in fostering a positive parent-child relationship. By prioritizing these aspects and nurturing a strong bond with their children, parents can help them grow into happy, healthy, and well-adjusted individuals. The benefits of a strong parent-child relationship extend far beyond childhood, laying the foundation for a lifetime of love, trust, and mutual respect.

• • • •

- IMPORTANCE OF COMMUNICATION in parenting

Effective communication is a crucial aspect of parenting that cannot be overlooked. It serves as the foundation for building a strong and healthy relationship between parents and their children. Communication involves not only the verbal exchange of information but also the non-verbal cues, such as body language and facial expressions, that convey important messages. By communicating openly and effectively with their children, parents can foster trust, understanding, and mutual respect in the parent-child relationship.

One of the key reasons why communication is important in parenting is that it allows parents to understand their children's thoughts, feelings, and needs. By actively listening to what their children have to say, parents can gain insight into their perspective and develop a deeper understanding of their unique personalities. This, in turn, helps parents to better meet their children's emotional and psychological needs, thus promoting their overall well-being and development.

Furthermore, communication plays a crucial role in setting boundaries and expectations for children. By clearly communicating rules, expectations, and consequences, parents can help children understand what is expected of them and why certain behaviors are not acceptable. Consistent communication about boundaries and expectations helps to establish a sense of structure and security for children, enabling them to develop self-discipline and self-regulation skills.

Effective communication in parenting also helps to build a strong parent-child bond. When parents communicate openly and honestly with their children, it fosters a sense of trust and connection that is essential for building a positive relationship. Children who feel supported and understood by their parents are more likely to confide in them, seek guidance, and turn to them for support in times of need. This bond not only strengthens the parent-child relationship but also provides a sense of security and stability for children as they navigate the challenges of growing up.

Moreover, communication in parenting plays a key role in promoting positive behavior and social skills in children. When parents communicate respectfully and constructively with their children, they serve as role models for effective communication and conflict resolution. By modeling healthy communication strategies, parents can teach their children how to express themselves assertively, listen actively, and resolve conflicts peacefully. These valuable social skills not only benefit children in their interactions with others but also contribute to their overall emotional intelligence and resilience.

In addition, effective communication in parenting helps to foster a sense of empowerment and autonomy in children. When parents communicate openly and encourage their children to express their thoughts and feelings, it sends a powerful message that their opinions and perspectives are valued. This validation of their individuality and autonomy helps children develop a sense of self-worth and confidence in their abilities, leading to greater independence and self-reliance as they grow and mature. By engaging in open, honest, and respectful communication with their children, parents can foster trust, understanding, and mutual respect in the parent-child relationship. Effective communication helps parents understand their children's thoughts, feelings, and needs, sets boundaries and expectations, builds a strong parent-child bond, promotes positive behavior and social skills, and empowers children to express themselves and develop a sense of autonomy. Ultimately, good communication is the key to creating a nurturing and supportive environment where children can thrive and reach their full potential.

- Active listening and empathy

Active listening and empathy are two key components of effective communication and building strong relationships. In today's fast-paced and often chaotic world, these skills are more important than ever in fostering understanding and connection with others. Active listening involves fully engaging with the speaker, showing interest and attentiveness, and providing feedback to ensure understanding. Empathy, on the other hand, involves putting oneself in someone else's shoes, understanding their perspective, and responding with compassion and understanding.

One of the key aspects of active listening is being fully present and engaged in the conversation. This means putting away distractions such as phones or other devices, making eye contact with the speaker, and nodding or providing verbal cues to show that you are listening. It also involves asking clarifying questions or paraphrasing what the speaker has said to ensure that you have understood their point of view. By actively listening in this way, you demonstrate to the speaker that you value their thoughts and feelings, which can help to build trust and rapport.

Empathy is closely related to active listening, as it involves truly understanding and connecting with the emotions and experiences of another person. This can be challenging, as it requires setting aside your own preconceived notions and biases in order to truly empathize with someone else's perspective. Empathy involves not only understanding someone else's feelings, but also responding in a caring and supportive way. This can help to validate the other person's emotions and experiences, and show that you are there to support them in a meaningful way.

Using active listening and empathy in communication can have a number of positive effects on relationships and interactions. When you actively listen to someone, it shows that you are attentive and interested in what they have to say, which can make them feel valued and respected. Similarly, when you respond with empathy and understanding, it can help to create a sense of connection and trust between you and the other person. This can lead to improved communication, more open and honest conversations, and stronger relationships overall.

In a professional context, active listening and empathy are essential skills for effective leadership and communication. By actively listening to employees, managers can better understand their concerns, ideas, and perspectives, which can lead to more informed decision-making and a more engaged and motivated workforce. Similarly, by responding with empathy and understanding, leaders can create a supportive and positive work environment, which can boost morale, productivity, and job satisfaction among employees.

In an academic setting, active listening and empathy are important for building rapport and understanding with students. By actively listening to students, teachers can better understand their learning needs and challenges, which can help to tailor instruction to better meet their needs. Similarly, by responding with empathy and understanding, teachers can create a supportive and inclusive classroom environment, which can help students feel valued and motivated to learn. This can lead to improved academic performance, increased student engagement, and a more positive overall learning experience for students. By actively listening to others and responding with empathy and understanding, we can create a supportive and positive environment that fosters trust, connection, and mutual respect. By developing these skills and incorporating them into our interactions with others, we can improve our communication, enhance our relationships, and create more meaningful and fulfilling connections with those around us.

- Setting clear expectations and boundaries

Setting clear expectations and boundaries is a crucial aspect of establishing effective communication and relationships in both personal and professional settings. By clearly defining what is expected of individuals and what behavior is acceptable or unacceptable, conflicts and misunderstandings can be minimized, and productivity and cooperation can be maximized. In this essay, we will explore the importance of setting clear expectations and boundaries, discuss some strategies for doing so effectively, and examine the positive impact that this practice can have on various aspects of life.

One of the primary reasons why setting clear expectations and boundaries is so critical is that it helps to prevent misunderstandings and conflicts. When everyone involved understands what is expected of them and what behavior is acceptable or unacceptable, there is less room for misinterpretation and disagreement. This clarity can reduce feelings of frustration and resentment, as individuals know exactly what is required of them and what they can expect from others. By setting clear expectations and boundaries, we can create a more harmonious and efficient environment where everyone is on the same page and working towards common goals.

In addition to avoiding conflicts and misunderstandings, setting clear expectations and boundaries can also help to improve communication and overall productivity. When individuals know what is expected of them, they can focus their efforts on meeting those expectations and delivering results. This clarity of purpose can enhance motivation and engagement, as individuals have a clear understanding of what they need to do to succeed. Furthermore, setting boundaries can help to define the roles and responsibilities of each person involved, leading to more efficient teamwork and collaboration. By establishing clear guidelines for communication and behavior, we can foster a more positive and productive work environment.

There are several strategies that can be employed to set clear expectations and boundaries effectively. One of the first steps is to clearly communicate expectations and boundaries to all individuals involved. This can be done through verbal communication, written guidelines, or formal agreements, depending on the situation. It is important to be specific and detailed in defining expectations and boundaries, leaving no room for ambiguity or confusion. By outlining what is expected of each person, as well as the consequences for failing to meet those expectations, we can ensure that everyone is on the same page and working towards a common goal.

Another strategy for setting clear expectations and boundaries is to lead by example. As a leader or supervisor, it is important to exemplify the behavior and attitudes that you expect from others. By demonstrating respect, professionalism, and accountability in your own actions, you can set a positive example for others to follow. Additionally, it is important to provide feedback and guidance to individuals when they are not meeting expectations or crossing boundaries. By addressing issues in a timely and respectful manner, you can help to correct behavior and prevent future problems.

The positive impact of setting clear expectations and boundaries can be seen in various aspects of life, including personal relationships, work environments, and educational settings. In personal relationships, establishing clear boundaries can help to define the parameters of the relationship and ensure that both individuals feel respected and valued. By communicating openly and honestly about expectations and boundaries, we can create a more harmonious and fulfilling relationship where both parties feel understood and supported. In work environments, setting clear expectations and boundaries can lead to improved communication, teamwork, and productivity. By defining roles and responsibilities, as well as outlining acceptable behavior and consequences, we can create a more efficient and positive work culture where everyone is working towards common goals. Similarly, in educational settings, setting clear expectations and boundaries can help to create a more structured and effective learning environment. By clearly communicating academic expectations and behavioral guidelines, educators can help students to succeed and reach their full potential. By clearly defining what is expected of individuals and what behavior is acceptable or unacceptable, conflicts, misunderstandings, and inefficiencies can be minimized, and productivity and cooperation can be maximized. By employing strategies such as clear communication, leading by example, and providing feedback, we can establish a more positive and structured environment where everyone feels respected and valued. The positive impact of setting clear expectations and boundaries can be seen in personal relationships, work environments, and educational settings, leading to improved communication, teamwork, and productivity. By prioritizing clarity and respect in our interactions, we can create a more harmonious and fulfilling environment where everyone can thrive.

• • • •

- DISCIPLINE VS. PUNISHMENT

Discipline and punishment are commonly used terms when it comes to correcting behavior and promoting positive growth and development, especially in educational and parenting contexts. However, these terms are often used interchangeably, leading to confusion about their meanings and implications. It is important to understand the differences between discipline and punishment in order to effectively address behavioral issues and promote positive outcomes.

Discipline can be defined as a systematic approach to teaching and guiding individuals towards desired behaviors and outcomes. It involves setting clear expectations, providing guidance and support, and using positive reinforcement to encourage positive behaviors. Discipline focuses on promoting self-control, responsibility, and accountability, and aims to foster intrinsic motivation and respect for rules and boundaries. In essence, discipline is about teaching individuals how to make the right choices and take responsibility for their actions.

On the other hand, punishment is a reactive approach to addressing misbehavior by imposing negative consequences for disobedience or rule-breaking. Punishment typically involves the use of punitive measures such as reprimands, loss of privileges, or physical consequences to deter unwanted behavior. While punishment may temporarily stop the unwanted behavior, it often fails to address the underlying causes of the behavior or teach individuals how to make better choices in the future. Punishment can also lead to negative emotions, resentment, and a lack of trust between the disciplinarian and the individual being punished.

One key difference between discipline and punishment is their underlying philosophy and goal. Discipline focuses on fostering positive behavior through learning and growth, while punishment is more concerned with providing retribution or retribution for wrongdoing. Discipline is proactive and preventative in nature, seeking to promote long-term positive outcomes and personal growth, while punishment is reactive and punitive, focusing on correcting behavior in the short term.

Another important distinction between discipline and punishment lies in their effectiveness and impact on behavior. Research has shown that discipline is more effective than punishment in promoting positive behavior and emotional well-being. Discipline helps individuals develop self-discipline, self-control, and problem-solving skills, leading to better decision-making and increased self-esteem. In contrast, punishment has been found to be less effective in changing behavior, as it often leads to resentment, defiance, and a lack of internal motivation to behave appropriately.

It is important for educators, parents, and caregivers to understand the differences between discipline and punishment and to choose the most effective approach when dealing with behavioral issues. Discipline is a more effective and sustainable approach to promoting positive behavior and personal growth, as it focuses on teaching individuals how to make positive choices and take responsibility for their actions. Punishment, on the other hand, may provide short-term compliance but is less likely to result in long-term behavioral change or personal development. Discipline focuses on teaching and guiding individuals towards positive behaviors through positive reinforcement and guidance, while punishment seeks to deter unwanted behaviors through negative consequences. Understanding the differences between discipline and punishment is crucial for promoting positive behavior and personal growth in educational and parenting contexts. By choosing discipline over punishment, educators, parents, and caregivers can help individuals develop self-control, responsibility, and empathy, leading to better decision-making and improved emotional well-being.

- Positive discipline strategies

Positive discipline strategies are crucial in shaping children's behavior and fostering a supportive environment for their growth and development. By focusing on positive reinforcement rather than punishment, these strategies aim to teach children about responsibility, self-control, and empathy. Research has shown that positive discipline techniques lead to more respectful and cooperative behavior in children, as well as stronger parent-child relationships. In this paper, we will discuss the key principles of positive discipline, highlight some effective strategies for implementing it, and explore its benefits for both children and parents.

One of the fundamental principles of positive discipline is the importance of building a strong relationship with the child based on trust and mutual respect. This means establishing clear communication channels, listening to the child's perspective, and validating their feelings. By fostering a positive and supportive connection, parents can create a safe space for their child to express themselves and learn from their mistakes. This relationship serves as the foundation for implementing positive discipline strategies effectively and reinforcing desired behaviors in the child.

Another key principle of positive discipline is the focus on teaching rather than punishing. Instead of using traditional disciplinary methods such as yelling, spanking, or time-outs, positive discipline advocates for positive reinforcement and logical consequences. When a child engages in inappropriate behavior, parents can use this as an opportunity to teach them about the impact of their actions and help them understand why certain behaviors are not acceptable. By focusing on teaching and guiding the child, parents can promote self-reflection and self-regulation, leading to long-term behavioral change.

Some effective positive discipline strategies include setting clear expectations and boundaries, using positive language and reinforcement techniques, and practicing empathy and understanding. By establishing clear rules and consequences, parents can provide their child with a sense of structure and predictability, which is crucial for promoting self-discipline and accountability. Using positive language and reinforcement techniques, such as praise, rewards, and incentives, can help motivate the child to exhibit positive behaviors and make better choices.

Empathy and understanding are also key components of positive discipline. By recognizing and validating the child's emotions, parents can cultivate a deeper connection with their child and help them regulate their emotions effectively. This can lead to improved communication, conflict resolution, and problem-solving skills in the child. By practicing empathy and understanding, parents can create a nurturing and supportive environment where the child feels safe and valued, enhancing their overall well-being and development.

The benefits of positive discipline extend beyond just shaping children's behavior. Research has shown that children who experience positive discipline are more likely to exhibit higher self-esteem, emotional intelligence, and social skills. They are also less likely to engage in risky behaviors, such as substance abuse or delinquency. Additionally, parents who practice positive discipline report higher levels of satisfaction in their parenting role and stronger parent-child relationships. By focusing on building trust and mutual respect, teaching rather than punishing, and practicing empathy and understanding, parents can create a positive and nurturing environment for their child to thrive. By implementing effective positive discipline techniques, parents can help their child develop important life skills such as empathy, self-control, and responsibility, setting them up for success both now and in the future.

- Teaching values and responsibility

Teaching values and responsibility is a crucial aspect of education that goes beyond academic success. In today's fast-paced and ever-changing world, it is essential for educators to instill in students a strong sense of values and responsibility that will guide them in making ethical decisions and navigating complex moral dilemmas. Values such as honesty, integrity, respect, empathy, and compassion play a pivotal role in shaping students' character and preparing them to be responsible members of society.

One of the key ways to teach values and responsibility in the classroom is through modeling behavior. Educators are role models for their students, and it is important for them to demonstrate the values they wish to instill in their students. By consistently exhibiting honesty, integrity, respect, and other positive values in their own actions and interactions, teachers can set a powerful example for their students to follow. Additionally, educators can create opportunities for students to practice these values in real-life situations, such as in group projects, classroom discussions, and community service projects.

Another effective strategy for teaching values and responsibility is through explicit instruction. Educators can incorporate lessons and activities that focus on specific values and principles, such as decision-making, conflict resolution, and ethical reasoning. By discussing hypothetical scenarios and case studies, students can develop critical thinking skills and learn how to apply values and responsibility in practical situations. In addition, educators can engage students in discussions about current events, social issues, and moral dilemmas to help them understand the importance of values and responsibility in the real world.

Furthermore, educators can cultivate a positive and supportive classroom environment that promotes values and responsibility. By encouraging open communication, collaboration, and teamwork among students, educators can foster a sense of community and mutual respect in the classroom. This sense of belonging and connection can motivate students to uphold values and take responsibility for their actions. Additionally, educators can provide opportunities for students to reflect on their own values and beliefs, and to set personal goals for growth and development.

In addition to teaching values and responsibility in the classroom, educators can involve parents, families, and the wider community in the process. By engaging parents and caregivers in discussions about values and responsibility, educators can create a unified support system that reinforces the importance of these qualities both at home and at school. Furthermore, educators can collaborate with community organizations, businesses, and other stakeholders to provide students with opportunities to practice values and responsibility in real-world settings, such as through internships, mentorship programs, and service-learning projects. By modeling positive behavior, providing explicit instruction, creating a supportive classroom environment, and involving parents and the community, educators can help students develop the values and skills they need to navigate the complexities of the modern world with integrity and compassion. Through these efforts, educators can prepare students to become ethical leaders and global citizens who contribute positively to society and make a lasting impact on the world around them.

Chapter 5: Encouraging Independence

- FOSTERING INDEPENDENCE and self-esteem

Fostering independence and self-esteem are crucial components of personal development and well-being. These two qualities go hand in hand, as individuals who possess a strong sense of independence are more likely to have high self-esteem, and vice versa. Independence refers to the ability to think and act for oneself, make decisions, and take responsibility for one's actions. Self-esteem, on the other hand, relates to the value and worth one places on themselves. When individuals feel capable, competent, and in control of their lives, they are more likely to have a positive self-esteem.

One of the key ways to foster independence and self-esteem is through encouraging and supporting individuals to take on new challenges and responsibilities. By allowing individuals to stretch themselves beyond their comfort zones, they can develop new skills, learn from their mistakes, and gain a sense of accomplishment that boosts their confidence. Providing opportunities for individuals to make decisions and solve problems on their own also helps to build independence and self-esteem. This can be done through assigning tasks that require critical thinking and decision-making, and providing guidance and feedback when needed.

Another important aspect of fostering independence and self-esteem is promoting a growth mindset. A growth mindset is the belief that one's abilities and intelligence can be developed through hard work, learning, and perseverance. By instilling a growth mindset in individuals, they are more likely to embrace challenges, learn from failures, and persist in the face of setbacks. This can help individuals build resilience, adaptability, and a sense of self-efficacy, which in turn boosts their self-esteem.

In addition to encouraging independence and promoting a growth mindset, it is important to provide individuals with opportunities for autonomy and self-expression. Allowing individuals to have a say in decisions that affect them, giving them choices and options, and respecting their needs and preferences help to nurture a sense of autonomy and empowerment. When individuals feel that they have control over their own lives and are able to express themselves freely, they are more likely to develop a positive self-image and self-esteem.

Individuals also benefit from positive and supportive relationships that foster independence and self-esteem. Being surrounded by people who believe in their abilities, provide encouragement and support, and offer constructive feedback can help individuals develop a sense of self-worth and confidence. Positive relationships can also provide a sense of belonging and connection, which are essential for overall well-being. Encouraging individuals to build strong social networks and seek out supportive relationships can help them feel valued, accepted, and understood, which in turn enhances their self-esteem.

To summarize, fostering independence and self-esteem requires creating a positive and nurturing environment that promotes growth, learning, and self-discovery. This includes providing clear expectations, setting realistic goals, and offering praise and recognition for achievements. It also involves creating a space where individuals feel safe to take risks, make mistakes, and learn from them without fear of judgment or criticism. By creating a supportive environment that values and celebrates individual strengths and differences, individuals are more likely to develop a strong sense of independence and self-esteem. By encouraging individuals to take on challenges, promoting a growth mindset, providing opportunities for autonomy and self-expression, nurturing positive relationships, and creating a supportive environment, we can help individuals develop the confidence, resilience, and self-worth they need to thrive. By investing in the development of independence and self-esteem, we can empower individuals to reach their full potential and lead fulfilling and meaningful lives.

- Age-appropriate responsibilities

Age-appropriate responsibilities refer to tasks and expectations that are suitable for individuals based on their age and level of development. These responsibilities are important for promoting independence, building self-esteem, and fostering a sense of contribution within the family or community. By assigning age-appropriate responsibilities, parents and educators can help children develop important life skills and values that will benefit them throughout their lives.

For young children, age-appropriate responsibilities may include simple tasks such as putting away toys, feeding pets, or helping to set the table. These tasks help children learn basic organizational and self-care skills, as well as the importance of contributing to the household. As children grow older, their responsibilities can be increased to include more complex tasks such as doing laundry, preparing meals, or mowing the lawn. By gradually increasing the level of responsibility assigned to children, parents and educators can help them build confidence and develop a sense of competence in their abilities.

It is important to consider a child's age, maturity, and individual abilities when assigning responsibilities. While it is important to challenge children and encourage them to take on new tasks, it is also important to ensure that the tasks are appropriate for their level of development. For example, a young child may not be ready to handle tasks that involve using sharp objects or navigating potentially dangerous situations. It is important for parents and educators to provide guidance and supervision as children take on new responsibilities, and to offer support and encouragement as they learn and grow.

Age-appropriate responsibilities can also help children develop important values such as responsibility, accountability, and perseverance. By taking on tasks and seeing them through to completion, children learn the value of hard work and the satisfaction that comes from completing a task successfully. They also learn the importance of taking ownership of their actions and the consequences that come with not fulfilling their responsibilities. By instilling these values early on, parents and educators can help children develop a strong work ethic and a sense of personal accountability that will serve them well in all aspects of their lives.

In addition to promoting important life skills and values, age-appropriate responsibilities can also help children develop a sense of autonomy and independence. By giving children tasks to complete on their own, parents and educators empower them to take ownership of their own lives and decisions. This sense of independence can help children develop self-confidence and a sense of agency, enabling them to navigate the challenges and opportunities that come their way with resilience and determination. By gradually increasing the level of responsibility assigned to children, parents and educators can help them build the skills and confidence necessary to become independent and self-reliant individuals. By assigning tasks that are suitable for a child's age and level of development, parents and educators can help children build important life skills, values, and a sense of independence. Through age-appropriate responsibilities, children learn the importance of contributing to their families and communities, taking ownership of their actions, and working hard to achieve their goals. By instilling these values early on, parents and educators can help prepare children for success in all aspects of their lives, fostering their growth and development into capable, responsible, and independent individuals.

- Allowing for mistakes and growth

Allowing for mistakes and growth is an essential aspect of both personal and professional development. It is through making mistakes that we learn and grow, ultimately becoming better versions of ourselves. In a society that often places a high value on perfection and success, it can be easy to feel discouraged when we make mistakes. However, it is important to remember that mistakes are a natural part of the learning process and should be embraced rather than feared.

When we allow ourselves and others to make mistakes, we create a safe and supportive environment for growth. Instead of being met with criticism and judgment, individuals are encouraged to reflect on their mistakes and learn from them. This type of environment fosters a growth mindset, where challenges are seen as opportunities for learning and development rather than obstacles to be avoided. By embracing mistakes, we can cultivate resilience and perseverance, traits that are essential for success in both personal and professional endeavors.

In the professional world, allowing for mistakes and growth can lead to increased innovation and creativity. When employees are given the freedom to take risks and make mistakes, they are more likely to think outside the box and come up with unconventional solutions to challenges. This type of environment fosters a culture of experimentation and continuous improvement, where mistakes are seen as valuable learning experiences rather than failures. As a result, companies that embrace a culture of learning and growth are better equipped to adapt to change and thrive in an ever-evolving marketplace.

It is also important for leaders to model the behavior of allowing for mistakes and growth. By admitting their own mistakes and demonstrating a willingness to learn and improve, leaders can create a culture where vulnerability is celebrated rather than stigmatized. This type of leadership can inspire others to take risks and push themselves out of their comfort zones, leading to increased creativity and innovation within the organization. Ultimately, leaders who embrace mistakes and growth are better able to empower their teams and drive success in their respective fields.

In our personal lives, allowing for mistakes and growth can lead to increased self-awareness and self-compassion. When we are able to acknowledge our mistakes without judgment, we can learn from them and make positive changes in our behavior. This type of introspection can lead to personal growth and development, ultimately allowing us to become the best versions of ourselves. By embracing mistakes as opportunities for growth rather than failures, we can cultivate a sense of resilience and self-confidence that empowers us to overcome challenges and achieve our goals. By creating a safe and supportive environment where mistakes are seen as valuable learning experiences, we can cultivate a growth mindset that empowers us to learn, adapt, and thrive in an ever-changing world. Leaders who model this behavior can inspire others to take risks and push themselves out of their comfort zones, leading to increased creativity and innovation within their organizations. Ultimately, by embracing mistakes as opportunities for growth, we can become more resilient, self-aware, and successful individuals.

Chapter 6: Building a Support System

• • • •

- IMPORTANCE OF A SUPPORT network

In today's fast-paced and high-pressure world, having a strong support network is more important than ever. A support network consists of people who are there for you in times of need, offering emotional support, practical assistance, and guidance. This network can include family members, friends, colleagues, neighbors, and even professionals such as therapists or counselors. The importance of having a support network cannot be overstated, as it can help you navigate the challenges of life, cope with stress, and achieve your goals.

One of the key benefits of having a support network is that it provides a sense of belonging and connection. Human beings are social creatures by nature, and we thrive when we have meaningful relationships with others. A support network can give you a sense of community and can help combat feelings of loneliness and isolation. Knowing that you have people you can turn to for help and support can provide a sense of security and comfort, as you know you are not facing life's challenges alone.

In addition to providing emotional support, a support network can also offer practical assistance when needed. Whether you need help moving, babysitting, or just someone to talk to, having a network of people you can rely on can make a big difference in your life. This practical support can help reduce stress and make it easier to navigate difficult situations. For example, if you are going through a divorce, having friends and family members who can help you with legal advice, emotional support, or even just a listening ear can make a world of difference.

Another important aspect of having a support network is that it can help you cope with stress and maintain your mental health. Life is full of ups and downs, and having people who can support you during tough times can be crucial for your well-being. Research has shown that social support can help reduce the negative effects of stress on both physical and mental health. By having people you can turn to for support, you can better cope with life's challenges and prevent feelings of overwhelm or burnout.

Having a support network can also help you achieve your goals and dreams. Whether you are working towards a career goal, trying to improve your health, or pursuing a personal passion, having people in your corner cheering you on can make all the difference. Your support network can provide encouragement, advice, and accountability to help you stay motivated and on track. They can also help you brainstorm ideas, connect you with resources, and provide valuable feedback to help you succeed. Whether you are facing a difficult situation, trying to cope with stress, or working towards a goal, having people you can turn to for help and support can make a big difference in your life. Building and maintaining a strong support network takes time and effort, but the benefits are well worth it. So reach out to your friends, family, colleagues, and other meaningful connections and nurture those relationships. Your support network can be a valuable resource that can help you navigate life's challenges, achieve your goals, and thrive in today's fast-paced world.

- Balancing work, family, and self-care

Balancing the demands of work, family, and self-care is a complex challenge that many individuals face in today's fast-paced society. Achieving a healthy equilibrium between these three essential aspects of life is crucial for overall well-being and success. It requires careful planning, time management, and prioritization to ensure that one is able to fulfill their responsibilities at work, nurture relationships with family members, and attend to their own physical and emotional needs.

At the heart of balancing work, family, and self-care is the concept of time management. Effectively managing one's time involves setting priorities, creating a schedule, and allocating time for each of the important aspects of life. One must identify the most critical tasks and responsibilities in each area and devote sufficient time and energy to them. This may involve making sacrifices or trade-offs in certain areas to ensure that all aspects of life are given the attention they deserve.

Prioritization is key when it comes to balancing work, family, and self-care. It is essential to identify the most important tasks and responsibilities in each area and focus on them first. This may require saying no to certain commitments or delegating tasks to others in order to free up time for what truly matters. By prioritizing effectively, one can ensure that they are able to fulfill their obligations at work, spend quality time with their family, and take care of themselves physically and emotionally.

Creating a schedule is another important aspect of balancing work, family, and self-care. By creating a schedule and sticking to it, one can ensure that they are able to allocate time for work, family activities, and self-care routines. This may involve setting aside specific blocks of time for each aspect of life and being disciplined about following the schedule. By having a clear plan in place, one can reduce stress, increase productivity, and make the most of their time.

In addition to time management, prioritization, and scheduling, self-care is an essential component of balancing work, family, and personal well-being. Taking care of oneself physically, emotionally, and mentally is crucial for overall health and happiness. This may involve engaging in activities that promote relaxation, stress relief, and overall well-being, such as exercise, meditation, hobbies, or spending time in nature. By prioritizing self-care, one can increase their energy levels, improve their mood, and enhance their ability to cope with the demands of work and family life.

Finding a balance between work, family, and self-care is an ongoing process that requires constant evaluation and adjustments. It is important to regularly assess how one is allocating their time and energy and make changes as needed to ensure that all aspects of life are being nurtured. This may involve seeking support from others, such as family members, friends, or colleagues, to help with tasks or responsibilities. By creating a support network and being open to asking for help, one can better manage the demands of work, family, and personal well-being. By effectively managing one's time, setting priorities, creating a schedule, and prioritizing self-care, one can achieve a healthy equilibrium between these three crucial aspects of life. By making conscious choices and being mindful of one's needs and limitations, one can ensure that they are able to fulfill their responsibilities at work, nurture relationships with family members, and attend to their own physical and emotional well-being. By finding a balance that works for them, individuals can lead fulfilling and successful lives both personally and professionally.

- Seeking help when needed

Seeking help when needed is an important aspect of personal growth and development. It is essential to recognize when we are facing challenges or difficulties that we are unable to overcome on our own, and to reach out for support from others. This can be in the form of seeking guidance from a mentor, counselor, or therapist, or simply asking for help from friends, family, or colleagues. By acknowledging our limitations and seeking assistance when needed, we can improve our chances of success and well-being.

One reason why seeking help when needed is so crucial is that it allows us to gain a fresh perspective on our situation. When we are facing a problem or struggling with a dilemma, it can be easy to become overwhelmed and lose sight of possible solutions. By seeking help from others, we can benefit from their insights and experiences, which may provide us with new ideas and strategies for addressing our challenges. This outside perspective can help us to see our situation more clearly and make more informed decisions about how to move forward.

Another important reason to seek help when needed is that it can help us to process and cope with difficult emotions. When we are going through a tough time, it is natural to experience a range of emotions, such as sadness, anxiety, or frustration. Seeking help from a counselor or therapist can provide us with a safe space to express and explore these emotions, which can help us to process and understand them better. This can be especially helpful for managing stress and anxiety, as talking to someone else about our feelings can help to alleviate some of the burden we may feel.

In addition to gaining a fresh perspective and processing difficult emotions, seeking help when needed can also help us to develop new skills and coping strategies. When we reach out for support from others, we may have the opportunity to learn from their experiences and insights, which can help us to build our own resilience and problem-solving abilities. For example, seeking guidance from a mentor or coach can help us to develop new skills in communication, time management, or conflict resolution. By being open to learning from others, we can expand our own knowledge and capabilities, which can benefit us in both our personal and professional lives.

It is important to recognize that seeking help when needed is not a sign of weakness, but rather a sign of strength and self-awareness. We all face challenges and struggles at some point in our lives, and it is natural to need support and assistance from others from time to time. By acknowledging our vulnerabilities and reaching out for help when needed, we are taking proactive steps to improve our own well-being and enhance our chances of success. This willingness to seek help demonstrates a willingness to learn and grow, which are valuable qualities that can benefit us in all areas of our lives. By acknowledging our limitations and reaching out for support from others, we can gain new perspectives, process difficult emotions, and develop new skills and coping strategies. It is important to remember that seeking help is not a sign of weakness, but rather a sign of strength and self-awareness. By being open to learning from others and seeking assistance when needed, we can improve our chances of success and well-being in all areas of our lives.

. . . .

- TEACHING EMOTIONAL intelligence

Emotional intelligence, often referred to as EQ, is a crucial skill set that encompasses the ability to understand and manage emotions effectively. It goes beyond simply being aware of one's own emotions; it also involves recognizing and responding to the emotions of others in a constructive manner.

One of the key components of emotional intelligence is self-awareness. This involves being able to recognize and understand one's own emotions, as well as how they may influence thoughts and behaviors. By cultivating self-awareness in students, we empower them to better understand themselves and how they react to different situations. This can help them to make more informed decisions and build healthier relationships with both peers and adults. Additionally, self-awareness can lead to increased motivation and resilience, as students are better equipped to navigate challenges and setbacks.

Another important aspect of emotional intelligence is self-regulation. This refers to the ability to manage and control one's emotions in a healthy and constructive way. Teaching students how to self-regulate not only fosters greater emotional stability, but it also promotes better decision-making and problem-solving skills. By learning how to pause and reflect before reacting impulsively, students can avoid unnecessary conflict and tension. This skill is particularly beneficial in academic settings, as it can help students maintain focus and stay on track with their studies.

In addition to self-awareness and self-regulation, social awareness is another crucial aspect of emotional intelligence. This involves the ability to empathize with others and understand their perspectives and feelings. By teaching students to be socially aware, we encourage them to develop stronger interpersonal skills and build more meaningful relationships. This can lead to improved collaboration and communication both in and out of the classroom. Social awareness also promotes a sense of inclusivity and respect for diversity, which are essential values in a globalized world.

Furthermore, relationship management is a key component of emotional intelligence that educators should prioritize teaching. This involves the ability to build and maintain positive and healthy relationships with others. By providing students with the necessary skills to manage relationships effectively, we help them navigate conflicts and disagreements with greater ease. Strong relationship management skills can also lead to enhanced teamwork and cooperation, which are essential in academic and professional settings. By fostering a sense of respect and understanding among students, educators can create a more supportive and inclusive learning environment. By prioritizing self-awareness, self-regulation, social awareness, and relationship management, educators can empower students to navigate the complexities of emotions and relationships with greater ease and confidence. By integrating emotional intelligence into our curriculum and classroom practices, we can create a more empathetic and understanding community that values emotional well-being alongside academic achievement. Ultimately, teaching emotional intelligence is an investment in the future success and happiness of our students.

- Coping with stress and challenges

Coping with stress and challenges is an essential skill that individuals must develop in order to navigate the complexities of life. In today's fast paced and demanding world, it is inevitable that we will encounter various stressors and obstacles that can disrupt our peace of mind and well-being. However, by learning effective coping strategies and techniques, we can better manage these stressors and challenges and maintain our mental and emotional stability.

One important aspect of coping with stress and challenges is understanding the sources of stress in our lives. By identifying the triggers that cause stress, we can take proactive steps to address them and mitigate their impact. This requires self-awareness and introspection to recognize patterns of behavior, thoughts, and emotions that contribute to our stress levels. For example, if a particular work environment or relationship is causing you stress, it may be necessary to set boundaries, communicate effectively, or seek support from others to alleviate the pressure.

In addition to identifying the sources of stress, it is essential to develop healthy coping mechanisms that can help us manage and reduce stress effectively. These coping strategies can vary from person to person, as what works for one individual may not work for another. Some common coping mechanisms include exercise, mindfulness and meditation, deep breathing techniques, journaling, and seeking support from friends, family, or mental health professionals. Engaging in activities that bring joy and fulfillment, such as hobbies or creative pursuits, can also help reduce stress and provide a sense of relief.

Another key component of coping with stress and challenges is building resilience, which is the ability to bounce back from setbacks and adversity. Resilience is not a fixed trait but rather a skill that can be developed and strengthened over time. By cultivating a positive mindset, cultivating a strong support network, and practicing self-care, we can enhance our resilience and improve our ability to cope with stress and challenges. Additionally, setting realistic goals, breaking tasks down into manageable steps, and staying organized can help us navigate difficult situations with more ease and confidence.

It is worth noting that coping with stress and challenges is not a one-size-fits-all solution. What works for one person may not work for another, and it may require some trial and error to find the most effective coping strategies for your individual needs and circumstances. It is also important to practice self-compassion and be patient with yourself as you navigate through challenging times. Remember, it is okay to ask for help and seek support when needed, as no one is expected to face life's difficulties alone. By identifying the sources of stress, developing healthy coping mechanisms, building resilience, and seeking support when needed, we can better navigate the ups and downs of life and emerge stronger and more resilient in the face of adversity. Remember that it is okay to not have all the answers or feel overwhelmed at times – what matters is how we respond to these challenges and continue to grow and thrive despite the obstacles that come our way.

- Building resilience in children

Resilience can be defined as the ability to bounce back from adversity, to adapt and thrive in the face of challenges and setbacks. It is a quality that can help children navigate the ups and downs of life with confidence and strength. Research has shown that children who possess resilience are better equipped to handle stress, develop healthy coping mechanisms, and maintain positive mental health.

There are several key factors that contribute to building resilience in children. One of the most important is the presence of a supportive and nurturing environment. Children who have caring and reliable adults in their lives, such as parents, teachers, and other caregivers, are more likely to develop resilience. These adults can provide guidance, encouragement, and a sense of security that helps children feel safe and supported in times of difficulty.

Another important factor in building resilience is helping children develop strong social and emotional skills. This includes teaching them how to regulate their emotions, communicate effectively, and solve problems creatively. By developing these skills, children are better able to navigate relationships, manage stress, and cope with challenges in a healthy and productive way.

It is also important to teach children the value of perseverance and determination. Encouraging children to set goals, take risks, and learn from their mistakes can help them develop a growth mindset. This mindset allows children to see challenges as opportunities for growth and learning, rather than as insurmountable obstacles. By fostering a sense of resilience, children can develop a positive attitude towards setbacks and failures, knowing that they have the ability to overcome them.

Building resilience in children also involves fostering a sense of autonomy and independence. Encouraging children to take on age-appropriate responsibilities, make decisions, and solve problems on their own can help them develop a sense of self-efficacy and confidence in their abilities. When children feel empowered to take control of their own lives, they are better equipped to face challenges and setbacks with resilience and determination.

In addition to these factors, fostering a sense of optimism and hope is essential for building resilience in children. Teaching children to focus on their strengths, believe in their abilities, and cultivate a positive outlook can help them maintain a sense of optimism even in the face of adversity. By instilling a sense of hope and positivity, children can develop the resilience to persevere through difficult times and emerge stronger and more resilient. By nurturing these qualities in children, parents, teachers, and caregivers can help them develop the resilience to navigate life's challenges with confidence and strength. Building resilience in children is a lifelong journey that begins in childhood and continues throughout adolescence and adulthood. With the right support and guidance, children can develop the tools and skills they need to thrive in the face of adversity and emerge as resilient, confident, and capable individuals.

Chapter 8: Promoting Healthy Relationships

* * * *

- MODELING HEALTHY RELATIONSHIPS

Healthy relationships are essential for overall well-being and happiness. When individuals are in healthy relationships, they experience greater emotional and psychological fulfillment, increased satisfaction with life, and improved physical health. However, achieving and maintaining healthy relationships requires effort, open communication, and a willingness to work through challenges together. In this discussion, we will explore the key components of modeling healthy relationships and how individuals can cultivate positive, meaningful connections with others.

One of the foundational elements of modeling healthy relationships is effective communication. Communication is the cornerstone of any successful relationship, allowing individuals to express their needs, desires, and concerns in a clear and respectful manner. In healthy relationships, communication is open, honest, and non-judgmental. It involves active listening, empathy, and the ability to express oneself authentically. When individuals communicate effectively with their partners, they build trust, deepen their connection, and strengthen their bond. By practicing good communication skills, individuals can avoid misunderstandings, conflicts, and potential breakdowns in their relationships.

Another important aspect of modeling healthy relationships is setting boundaries. Boundaries are essential for establishing a sense of safety, respect, and autonomy within a relationship. Healthy boundaries help individuals define their personal limits, expectations, and values, and communicate them to their partners in a clear and assertive manner. By setting boundaries, individuals can protect themselves from harm, maintain their individuality, and foster mutual respect and understanding in their relationships. Setting and respecting boundaries is crucial for creating a healthy dynamic in which both partners feel heard, valued, and supported.

In addition to effective communication and setting boundaries, trust is a key component of modeling healthy relationships. Trust is the belief that one can rely on another person, feel safe with them, and be vulnerable without fear of betrayal or judgment. Trust is built through consistent behavior, open communication, and honesty. When individuals trust their partners, they feel secure, valued, and respected, which fosters intimacy, emotional connection, and a sense of partnership. By cultivating trust in their relationships, individuals can deepen their bond, strengthen their emotional connection, and create a lasting foundation for a healthy, fulfilling partnership.

Respect is another crucial element of modeling healthy relationships. Respect is the acknowledgment and acceptance of each other's individuality, values, and perspectives. In healthy relationships, partners treat each other with kindness, consideration, and understanding. They listen to each other's opinions, validate each other's feelings, and support each other's goals and aspirations. When individuals respect their partners, they create a positive environment that promotes mutual appreciation, empathy, and collaboration. By demonstrating respect in their relationships, individuals can foster a sense of equality, trust, and harmony that strengthens their bond and promotes a healthy, supportive partnership.

Furthermore, mutual support is essential for modeling healthy relationships. Partners in healthy relationships support each other's growth, well-being, and personal development. They encourage each other to pursue their goals, overcome challenges, and fulfill their potential. Mutual support involves active listening, empathy, and encouragement. When individuals feel supported by their partners, they feel validated, empowered, and motivated to achieve their goals. By offering and receiving support in their relationships, individuals can create a sense of teamwork, collaboration, and shared success that enhances their connection and strengthens their bond. By cultivating effective communication, setting boundaries, building trust, demonstrating respect, and offering mutual support, individuals can create meaningful, fulfilling connections with others. Healthy relationships are essential for promoting emotional well-being, enhancing life satisfaction, and improving overall health. By modeling healthy relationships, individuals can create a positive, supportive environment that fosters growth, connection, and happiness for themselves and their partners.

- Teaching empathy and respect

Empathy and respect are two crucial values that form the foundation of positive relationships, both in the classroom and beyond. As educators, it is our responsibility to cultivate these values in our students through intentional teaching and modeling. By fostering empathy, we help students understand and connect with the feelings and experiences of others, while respect teaches them to treat everyone with dignity and kindness. Together, these values create a safe and inclusive learning environment where all students feel valued and supported.

Teaching empathy begins with helping students develop an awareness of their own emotions and how their actions can impact others. Through activities such as role-playing, discussions, and reflective writing, students can explore different perspectives and practice responding empathetically to various situations. By encouraging students to listen actively, validate others' feelings, and consider alternative viewpoints, educators can help them build the empathy skills necessary for forming meaningful relationships and resolving conflicts effectively.

Respect is another essential value that should be embedded in the fabric of the classroom culture. By setting clear expectations for respectful behavior and consistently reinforcing these expectations through positive reinforcement and consequences, educators can create a respectful and inclusive learning environment. Additionally, incorporating lessons on diversity, equity, and inclusion can help students understand the importance of respecting and valuing the experiences and identities of others. By promoting respect for all individuals, regardless of differences, educators can foster a culture of mutual understanding and acceptance within the classroom.

In addition to explicit teaching of empathy and respect, educators must also model these values in their own behavior. By demonstrating empathy and respect in their interactions with students, colleagues, and parents, educators set a powerful example for their students to follow. Moreover, educators can use real-world examples and stories to illustrate the importance of empathy and respect in various contexts, helping students see how these values can positively impact individuals and communities.

Furthermore, educators can integrate lessons on empathy and respect across various subject areas, connecting these values to academic content and real-world issues. By incorporating literature, history, science, and other disciplines into discussions on empathy and respect, educators can help students see the relevance of these values in their daily lives and future careers. Additionally, educators can collaborate with other professionals, such as school counselors and social workers, to provide additional support and resources for students who may be struggling to develop empathy and respect. By intentionally teaching and modeling these values, educators can help students develop the social and emotional skills necessary for building strong relationships and navigating the complexities of the world around them. Through fostering empathy and respect in students, educators contribute to the creation of a more compassionate and tolerant society, where individuals treat each other with dignity and kindness. By prioritizing empathy and respect in our classrooms, we can create a more harmonious and equitable world for future generations to come.

- Addressing conflicts and challenges

Addressing conflicts and challenges is an essential skill in both personal and professional settings. Conflict is inevitable and can arise in any situation where there are differing opinions, goals, or values. By learning how to effectively address conflicts and challenges, individuals can improve their relationships, enhance their problem-solving skills, and create a more positive and productive work environment.

One of the first steps in addressing conflicts and challenges is to recognize and acknowledge the existence of the conflict. This may involve open and honest communication with the parties involved, and a willingness to listen to different perspectives. By acknowledging the conflict, individuals can begin to work towards finding a resolution and moving forward in a constructive manner.

Once the conflict has been acknowledged, it is important to identify the underlying issues that are contributing to the conflict. This may involve exploring the root causes of the conflict, such as differences in values, communication styles, or expectations. By understanding the underlying issues, individuals can work towards finding solutions that address the core of the conflict, rather than simply addressing the symptoms.

Communication is key in addressing conflicts and challenges. Effective communication involves listening to others, expressing one's own thoughts and feelings clearly, and working towards finding a mutual understanding. By communicating openly and honestly, individuals can ensure that their perspectives are heard and can work towards finding common ground.

In some cases, conflicts and challenges may require the assistance of a neutral third party, such as a mediator or facilitator. These individuals can help facilitate communication, guide the parties towards a resolution, and ensure that the conflict is addressed in a fair and equitable manner. By utilizing the services of a neutral third party, individuals can find creative and effective solutions to their conflicts.

It is important to approach conflicts and challenges with a positive attitude and a willingness to find a resolution. Conflict can be an opportunity for growth and learning, and by approaching conflicts with an open mind, individuals can work towards finding solutions that are mutually beneficial. Additionally, by staying positive and focused on finding a resolution, individuals can create a more positive and productive work environment. By acknowledging the conflict, identifying the underlying issues, communicating effectively, and utilizing the services of a neutral third party when necessary, individuals can work towards finding creative and effective solutions to their conflicts. By approaching conflicts with a positive attitude and a willingness to find a resolution, individuals can create a more positive and productive work environment and enhance their problem-solving skills.

• • • •

- TEACHING ACCEPTANCE and inclusivity

In today's diverse and ever-evolving society, it is essential for educators to prioritize teaching acceptance and inclusivity within the classroom. By creating a safe and welcoming environment for all students, regardless of their background, beliefs, or abilities, teachers can foster a sense of belonging and respect among their students. This not only promotes positive social interactions and relationships but also helps to cultivate a deeper understanding and appreciation for diversity.

Teaching acceptance and inclusivity goes beyond simply promoting tolerance; it involves actively embracing and celebrating the differences among students. It is important for educators to model inclusive behavior and language, as well as provide opportunities for students to engage in discussions and activities that highlight the value of diversity. By encouraging students to share their own experiences and perspectives, teachers can create a sense of community and mutual respect within the classroom.

One of the key aspects of promoting acceptance and inclusivity is to address and challenge stereotypes and biases that may exist within the classroom. Educators can do this by incorporating diverse perspectives and voices in the curriculum, as well as by providing resources and support for students who may feel marginalized or excluded. By promoting dialogue and reflection on issues of social justice and equality, teachers can help students develop a more critical and empathetic understanding of the world around them.

Another important aspect of teaching acceptance and inclusivity is to support students with diverse learning needs and abilities. Educators can do this by providing accommodations and modifications that allow all students to fully participate in classroom activities and discussions. By creating a learning environment that is accessible and responsive to the needs of all students, teachers can empower them to reach their full potential and contribute meaningfully to the classroom community. By fostering a culture of acceptance and respect within the classroom, educators can create a foundation for lifelong learning and positive social change. Through intentional and thoughtful practices, teachers can help students develop the skills and attitudes necessary to navigate an increasingly diverse and interconnected world with empathy, understanding, and inclusivity.

- Celebrating differences

Celebrating differences is an important aspect of fostering diversity and inclusivity in any society. Recognizing and appreciating the unique qualities and perspectives that each individual brings to the table can lead to a more harmonious and productive community. By embracing diversity, we are able to broaden our horizons, challenge our own biases, and learn from one another's experiences.

One of the key benefits of celebrating differences is the opportunity for personal growth and development. When we interact with people who have different backgrounds, beliefs, and viewpoints than our own, we are forced to confront our own preconceived notions and expand our understanding of the world. This can lead to increased empathy, tolerance, and acceptance of others. In a world that is becoming increasingly interconnected, it is more important than ever to be able to communicate and collaborate with individuals from diverse backgrounds.

Another important aspect of celebrating differences is the promotion of innovation and creativity. When people from different walks of life come together, they bring with them a wealth of knowledge, skills, and ideas that can lead to breakthrough solutions to complex problems. By fostering a culture of diversity and inclusivity, organizations can tap into the full potential of their workforce and drive innovation. Research has shown that diverse teams are more creative, more efficient, and more successful than homogenous groups.

Additionally, celebrating differences can help to break down barriers and eliminate stereotypes that can lead to discrimination and prejudice. By promoting understanding and respect for all individuals, regardless of their race, gender, sexual orientation, or abilities, we can create a more just and equitable society. This can lead to greater opportunities for social and economic mobility for marginalized communities, as well as a more cohesive and united society as a whole. By embracing diversity and inclusivity, we can create a more vibrant, dynamic, and innovative society that benefits all of its members. It is important to recognize the value that each individual brings to the table and to foster an environment in which everyone can thrive. By acknowledging and celebrating our differences, we can build a more harmonious and prosperous world for future generations.

- Creating a culture of respect

Creating a culture of respect within an organization is vital for ensuring a positive and inclusive work environment. Respect is the foundation of strong relationships and fosters collaboration, trust, and open communication among team members. When individuals feel respected, they are more likely to be engaged, motivated, and productive in their roles. Cultivating a culture of respect requires deliberate effort and commitment from both leaders and employees.

One of the key aspects of creating a culture of respect is promoting diversity and inclusion within the organization. By valuing and celebrating the unique perspectives, backgrounds, and experiences of all team members, organizations can create a more dynamic and innovative work environment. Inclusive practices such as listening to diverse viewpoints, actively seeking out feedback from all team members, and ensuring equal opportunities for growth and development can help establish a culture of respect where everyone feels valued and empowered to contribute.

Leaders play a crucial role in setting the tone for a culture of respect within an organization. It is essential for leaders to model respectful behavior and hold themselves and others accountable for upholding the organization's values. By demonstrating empathy, effective communication, and a willingness to listen to diverse perspectives, leaders can create a culture where respect is embedded in the organization's DNA. Establishing clear policies and procedures for addressing disrespectful behavior and promoting a zero-tolerance approach to harassment and discrimination are also essential steps in building a culture of respect.

In addition to leadership, employees must also play a role in cultivating a culture of respect within the organization. By treating colleagues, clients, and stakeholders with kindness, empathy, and professionalism, employees can contribute to a positive work environment where everyone feels respected and valued. Building strong relationships with coworkers, fostering a sense of teamwork and collaboration, and actively supporting inclusivity initiatives can help create a culture of respect that benefits not only the organization but also its employees.

Effective communication is another key component of creating a culture of respect within an organization. By fostering open and transparent communication channels, leaders and employees can ensure that all team members feel heard, valued, and understood. Encouraging feedback, actively listening to concerns, and addressing issues promptly and constructively can help prevent misunderstandings and conflicts from escalating and promote a culture of respect where everyone's voice is heard and respected.

To culminate, promoting a culture of respect also involves recognizing and celebrating individual and team achievements. By acknowledging and rewarding the contributions of team members, organizations can show appreciation and gratitude for their hard work and dedication. Recognizing diverse talents, skills, and accomplishments can help build a sense of pride, loyalty, and camaraderie within the organization and reinforce a culture of respect where everyone's contributions are valued and celebrated. By promoting diversity and inclusion, modeling respectful behavior, fostering open communication, and recognizing individual and team achievements, organizations can cultivate a positive and inclusive work environment where everyone feels respected, valued, and empowered. Building a culture of respect is not only beneficial for the organization's success but also for the well-being and satisfaction of its employees. By prioritizing respect and inclusivity, organizations can create a positive and supportive workplace culture that enables team members to thrive and achieve their full potential.

Chapter 10: Encouraging Lifelong Learning

• • • •

- FOSTERING A LOVE OF learning

Fostering a love of learning is essential for the success and well-being of students. When students are enthusiastic about learning, they are more motivated to explore new concepts, engage in critical thinking, and develop a deeper understanding of the world around them. As educators, it is our responsibility to create an environment that encourages curiosity, creativity, and a growth mindset. By cultivating a love of learning in our students, we are not only preparing them for academic success but also equipping them with the skills and mindset needed to thrive in an ever-changing world.

One of the most effective ways to foster a love of learning is to provide students with opportunities for hands-on, experiential learning. When students are actively engaged in their learning, they are more likely to retain information and develop a deeper understanding of the material. Experiential learning allows students to apply their knowledge in real-world situations, which can help them see the relevance and importance of what they are learning. By incorporating hands-on activities, experiments, and projects into the curriculum, educators can create a dynamic and engaging learning environment that inspires students to explore, create, and imagine.

Another key aspect of fostering a love of learning is to provide students with opportunities for choice and autonomy. When students have the freedom to pursue their interests and passions, they are more likely to be engaged and motivated in their learning. Giving students the opportunity to choose their own topics for research projects, select books for independent reading, or design their own experiments can empower them to take ownership of their learning and develop a sense of agency. By honoring students' interests and allowing them to make decisions about their learning, educators can create a learning environment that is more student-centered and personalized, which can lead to increased motivation and engagement.

In addition to providing hands-on experiences and opportunities for choice, educators can foster a love of learning by creating a supportive and nurturing classroom environment. When students feel safe, valued, and respected, they are more likely to take risks, ask questions, and engage in meaningful dialogue with their peers. Building positive relationships with students, providing encouragement and feedback, and creating a sense of belonging and community in the classroom can help to create a culture of learning that is inclusive, supportive, and affirming. By fostering a sense of trust and rapport with students, educators can create a learning environment that is conducive to exploration, creativity, and growth.

Furthermore, it is important for educators to model a love of learning themselves. When teachers demonstrate a passion for their subject matter, a curiosity about the world, and a commitment to lifelong learning, they can inspire their students to do the same. By sharing their own experiences of learning, failures, and successes, educators can show students that learning is a continuous and rewarding process that is worth pursuing. Modeling traits such as resilience, perseverance, and intellectual curiosity can help to instill a love of learning in students and demonstrate the value of education as a lifelong pursuit. By providing students with hands-on experiences, opportunities for choice, a supportive classroom environment, and by modeling a love of learning ourselves, educators can create a learning environment that is engaging, empowering, and inspiring. By nurturing students' curiosity, creativity, and passion for learning, we can help them develop the skills and mindset needed to succeed in school and in life. Ultimately, fostering a love of learning is not just about acquiring knowledge, but about developing a love of exploration, discovery, and intellectual growth that can last a lifetime.

- Supporting education and curiosity

Education is a fundamental cornerstone of society, as it shapes the minds and perspectives of individuals while providing them with the knowledge and skills needed to navigate the complexities of the world. It is through education that individuals gain critical thinking abilities, communication skills, and a deeper understanding of the world around them. However, education is not limited to traditional academic settings; it encompasses a broad spectrum of learning experiences that can occur in various environments. As such, it is crucial to support education in all its forms and encourage curiosity among learners of all ages.

One of the key ways to support education and foster curiosity is by creating a conducive learning environment that encourages exploration and discovery. This includes providing access to resources such as books, technology, and educational tools that can help individuals deepen their understanding of various subjects. Additionally, creating spaces for collaboration and discussion can enhance the learning experience, as it allows individuals to engage with diverse perspectives and exchange ideas. By creating an inclusive and supportive learning environment, educators can help cultivate a passion for learning and encourage curiosity among students.

Furthermore, supporting education and curiosity requires promoting a love for learning that goes beyond the traditional classroom setting. This can be achieved through extracurricular activities, community programs, and lifelong learning opportunities that allow individuals to explore their interests and passions. By providing opportunities for individuals to pursue their interests outside of formal education, we can help cultivate a lifelong love for learning and support curiosity in all its forms. Whether it be through art, music, sports, or other interests, fostering a sense of curiosity can lead to a more fulfilling and enriching life.

In addition to creating a conducive learning environment and promoting a love for learning, it is essential to support educators in their efforts to cultivate curiosity among their students. Teachers play a critical role in shaping the educational experience of students and can inspire curiosity through their passion for teaching and dedication to their students' learning. By providing educators with professional development opportunities, resources, and support, we can help them strengthen their teaching practices and create engaging learning experiences that promote curiosity and critical thinking skills.

Moreover, supporting education and curiosity also involves empowering individuals to take control of their learning journey and pursue their interests with confidence and curiosity. This can be achieved through mentorship programs, career guidance, and personalized learning plans that cater to the unique needs and interests of individuals. By providing individuals with the tools and support they need to pursue their passions, we can help them develop a lifelong love for learning and foster a sense of curiosity that drives them to explore new ideas and perspectives. By creating a conducive learning environment, promoting a love for learning, supporting educators, and empowering individuals to pursue their interests, we can help cultivate a culture of curiosity that inspires individuals to explore the world around them and engage with new ideas. Through these efforts, we can support education in all its forms and empower individuals to become lifelong learners who are curious, engaged, and passionate about learning.

- Embracing new experiences and challenges

Embracing new experiences and challenges is an essential part of personal growth and development. It is through stepping out of our comfort zones that we push ourselves to learn new things, adapt to different situations, and ultimately become more resilient individuals. While it may be daunting to face the unknown, it is important to remember that with each new experience comes an opportunity for growth and self-discovery.

One of the key benefits of embracing new experiences and challenges is the opportunity to expand our horizons and broaden our perspectives. By exposing ourselves to different people, cultures, and ideas, we open ourselves up to new ways of thinking and being in the world. This can lead to greater empathy, understanding, and tolerance, as we come to see the world from different vantage points. In a rapidly changing and interconnected world, the ability to adapt to new experiences and challenges is becoming increasingly important in order to thrive and succeed.

Another important aspect of embracing new experiences and challenges is the opportunity for personal development and skill enhancement. When we push ourselves to try new things and take on unfamiliar challenges, we are forced to confront our fears, overcome obstacles, and develop new skills and competencies. This can lead to increased self-confidence, self-efficacy, and a sense of accomplishment as we expand our capabilities and push the boundaries of what we thought was possible. Whether it's learning a new language, taking up a new hobby, or stepping into a leadership role, each new experience presents an opportunity for personal growth and development.

Additionally, embracing new experiences and challenges can lead to increased creativity and innovation. When we expose ourselves to new stimuli and ideas, our brains are forced to make new connections and think in new ways. This can lead to the generation of novel ideas, creative solutions, and innovative approaches to problems. By pushing ourselves outside of our comfort zones and embracing new challenges, we can stimulate our creativity and tap into our full potential as individuals. This can have far-reaching effects in both our personal and professional lives, as we become more adaptable, flexible, and open to new possibilities. By stepping out of our comfort zones, we can expand our horizons, enhance our skills, foster creativity, and ultimately become more resilient individuals. While it may be intimidating to face the unknown, it is important to remember that with each new experience comes an opportunity for growth and self-discovery. So, I encourage you to embrace new experiences and challenges with an open mind and a willingness to learn, grow, and evolve as individuals.

• • • •

- SETTING LIMITS ON screen time

Setting limits on screen time is a topic that has garnered significant attention in recent years, due to the proliferation of digital devices and the impact they can have on individuals' health and well-being. While screens have become an integral part of daily life for many people, excessive use can lead to a variety of negative consequences, including eye strain, disrupted sleep patterns, and a sedentary lifestyle. As a result, experts recommend establishing clear boundaries and guidelines for screen time to help mitigate these risks.

One of the key reasons to set limits on screen time is to promote a healthy balance between technology use and other activities. Prolonged periods of screen time can lead to a host of physical and mental health issues, including obesity, poor posture, and increased feelings of anxiety and depression. By establishing limits on screen time, individuals can ensure that they are prioritizing activities that promote their overall well-being, such as physical exercise, social interaction, and outdoor play.

In addition to promoting a healthier lifestyle, setting limits on screen time can also help to improve productivity and focus. Research has shown that excessive screen time can impair cognitive function and attention span, making it more difficult to concentrate on tasks and retain information. By limiting the amount of time spent on electronic devices, individuals can enhance their ability to concentrate, be more present in the moment, and improve their overall productivity in work and school.

Another important reason to set limits on screen time is to establish healthy boundaries around technology use within the family unit. With the ever-increasing availability of screens and digital devices, it can be challenging for parents to monitor and regulate their children's screen time effectively. By implementing clear guidelines for screen time usage, parents can help to create a healthier balance between technology and other activities, such as reading, playing outside, and spending quality time together as a family.

When setting limits on screen time, it is important to consider the specific needs and circumstances of each individual or family. While there are general guidelines recommended by experts, such as limiting screen time to no more than two hours per day for children and adolescents, it is crucial to tailor these recommendations to fit the unique needs and priorities of each individual. For example, some individuals may require more screen time for work or school-related activities, while others may benefit from stricter limits to prevent excessive use.

In order to effectively set limits on screen time, it is crucial to communicate openly and honestly about the reasons behind the restrictions and involve all family members in the decision-making process. By having a frank discussion about the potential risks of excessive screen time and the benefits of setting limits, individuals can better understand the rationale behind the guidelines and be more motivated to adhere to them. Additionally, by involving children and adolescents in the process, parents can help to foster a sense of responsibility and awareness around their own technology use. By establishing clear guidelines for technology use, individuals can reduce the risk of negative health consequences, improve their overall productivity and focus, and create healthy boundaries around technology within the family unit. By communicating openly and involving all family members in the decision-making process, individuals can work together to create a harmonious balance between screen time and other activities that support their well-being.

- Teaching digital citizenship

Digital citizenship is a vital concept for educators, parents, and students to understand in today's technologically advanced world. As technology continues to play a significant role in our daily lives, it is essential for individuals to be well-versed in how to navigate the digital landscape responsibly and ethically. Teaching digital citizenship refers to educating individuals on how to use technology in a safe, respectful, and responsible manner. It encompasses a variety of skills and knowledge, including online safety, digital literacy, cyberbullying prevention, and ethical behavior online. By teaching digital citizenship, educators can empower students to make informed decisions and engage with technology in a positive and productive way.

One of the key aspects of teaching digital citizenship is educating students on how to stay safe online. This includes teaching them about the importance of protecting their personal information, avoiding suspicious websites, and recognizing online scams. Students should also be taught about the potential dangers of social media and the importance of maintaining privacy settings on their accounts. By instilling good online safety practices in students, educators can help them navigate the digital world with confidence and avoid falling victim to cybercrimes or online predators.

In addition to online safety, digital citizenship education also involves teaching students about digital literacy. This includes teaching them how to evaluate the credibility of online sources, differentiate between fact and opinion, and navigate the vast amount of information available on the internet. Digital literacy skills are crucial in today's digital age, as individuals are constantly bombarded with information from a variety of sources. By teaching students how to critically assess and analyze information online, educators can help them become more informed and discerning digital citizens.

Cyberbullying prevention is another important aspect of teaching digital citizenship. Cyberbullying refers to the use of electronic communication to harass, intimidate, or threaten others. Educators should teach students about the negative impact of cyberbullying and how to recognize, prevent, and respond to it. By promoting a culture of kindness and respect online, educators can help create a safer and more inclusive digital environment for students. Encouraging students to speak up and report instances of cyberbullying is essential in addressing this pervasive issue and fostering a positive online community.

Teaching digital citizenship also involves educating students on ethical behavior online. This includes teaching them about the importance of respecting intellectual property rights, citing sources properly, and engaging in respectful and constructive online communication. Students should be taught about the consequences of plagiarism, copyright infringement, and online harassment. By instilling values of integrity, honesty, and respect in students, educators can help them become responsible digital citizens who contribute positively to online communities. By educating students on online safety, digital literacy, cyberbullying prevention, and ethical behavior online, educators can help empower them to make informed decisions and engage with technology in a positive and productive way. Promoting a culture of digital citizenship in schools and communities is essential in creating a safer and more inclusive digital environment for all individuals. By working together to educate and empower students to be responsible digital citizens, we can help shape a better and more positive digital future for generations to come.

- Promoting healthy tech habits

Promoting healthy tech habits is essential in today's digital age, where technology plays a significant role in our daily lives. With the increasing reliance on technology for communication, work, and entertainment, it is crucial to develop good habits that promote a healthy balance between tech use and other aspects of life. This can help prevent negative consequences such as digital addiction, eye strain, poor posture, and mental health issues.

One of the key aspects of promoting healthy tech habits is establishing boundaries and limits on tech use. Setting specific times for tech-free activities, such as meals, exercise, and relaxation, can help create a balanced lifestyle. Additionally, taking regular breaks from screens and being mindful of how much time is spent on devices can prevent overuse and potential negative effects on physical and mental health. By creating a schedule that includes dedicated time away from technology, individuals can better prioritize their well-being and reduce the risk of developing unhealthy habits.

Another important aspect of promoting healthy tech habits is practicing good digital hygiene. This includes maintaining a clean and organized digital workspace, backing up important files regularly, and updating software and security settings to protect against cyber threats. By taking proactive measures to safeguard personal information and devices, individuals can reduce the risk of data breaches, identity theft, and other security issues. Additionally, practicing digital hygiene can help improve efficiency and productivity by minimizing distractions and streamlining workflow.

In addition to setting boundaries and practicing good digital hygiene, promoting healthy tech habits also involves prioritizing self-care and well-being. This includes prioritizing sleep, exercise, and relaxation to recharge and refresh both the body and the mind. By prioritizing self-care and setting aside time for activities that nourish the body and mind, individuals can better balance their tech use and maintain a healthy lifestyle.

Furthermore, promoting healthy tech habits also involves cultivating mindfulness and awareness around tech use. This includes being conscious of how technology is impacting daily life and developing the ability to recognize when tech use becomes excessive or detrimental. By practicing mindfulness, individuals can better regulate their tech use and make intentional choices about when and how to engage with technology. By setting boundaries, practicing good digital hygiene, prioritizing self-care, and cultivating mindfulness, individuals can create a healthy relationship with technology that enhances well-being and supports personal growth. With the right habits and mindset, it is possible to harness the benefits of technology while avoiding the pitfalls of excessive use.

Chapter 12: Practicing Mindful Parenting

. . . .

- MINDFULNESS TECHNIQUES for parents

Mindfulness has become a popular practice in recent years, with many people turning to it as a way to manage stress, improve focus, and cultivate a greater sense of well-being. While mindfulness is often associated with meditation and yoga, it can also be a valuable tool for parents looking to navigate the many challenges of raising children. In this article, we will explore some mindfulness techniques that parents can use to help them stay calm, focused, and present in the midst of the chaos that often comes with parenting.

One of the key principles of mindfulness is being fully present in the moment, without judgment or distraction. For parents, this can be particularly challenging, as there are often a million things vying for their attention at any given time. However, by practicing mindfulness, parents can learn to focus on the present moment and let go of worries about the past or future. This can help them to be more attuned to their children's needs and respond to them in a more compassionate and effective way.

One simple mindfulness technique that parents can use is the practice of mindful breathing. This involves taking a few moments to focus on the sensation of breathing in and out, and letting go of any thoughts or distractions that may arise. By bringing their attention to their breath, parents can create a sense of calm and centeredness that can help them to better handle the ups and downs of parenting. Mindful breathing can be done at any time, whether it's in the midst of a tantrum or during a quiet moment alone.

Another mindfulness technique that can be especially helpful for parents is mindful listening. This involves giving your full attention to your child when they are speaking, without interrupting or trying to solve their problems. By truly listening to your child with an open mind and heart, you can create a deeper connection with them and show them that you value their thoughts and feelings. Mindful listening can also help parents to be more patient and empathetic, leading to better communication and stronger relationships with their children.

Mindfulness can also be a valuable tool for parents when it comes to managing their own emotions and reactions. Parenting can be an emotional rollercoaster, with feelings of frustration, guilt, and exhaustion often coming to the surface. By practicing mindfulness, parents can learn to observe their emotions without getting caught up in them, allowing them to respond to challenging situations in a more calm and intentional way. This can help to break the cycle of reacting impulsively and can lead to more positive outcomes for both parents and children.

In addition to these techniques, parents can also incorporate mindfulness into their daily routine by setting aside time for formal meditation practice. This can be as simple as taking a few minutes each day to sit quietly and focus on the breath, or it can involve more structured practices such as guided meditations or body scans. By making time for mindfulness practice, parents can cultivate a greater sense of self-awareness and emotional resilience, which can help them to be more effective and compassionate parents. By incorporating mindfulness techniques into their daily lives, parents can cultivate a greater sense of presence, compassion, and emotional resilience that can help them to be more attuned to their children's needs and respond to them in a more calm and effective way. So, next time you find yourself feeling overwhelmed or stressed out as a parent, remember to take a moment to breathe, listen, and connect with the present moment. Your children will thank you for it.

- Teaching mindfulness to children

Teaching mindfulness to children is a valuable practice that can have far-reaching benefits for their emotional and cognitive development. Mindfulness is the practice of being present and fully engaged in the moment, without judgment. By teaching children mindfulness techniques, we are equipping them with valuable tools to help them navigate the challenges of childhood and adolescence with grace and resilience.

One of the key benefits of teaching mindfulness to children is that it can help them manage stress and anxiety. In today's fast-paced world, children are constantly bombarded with stimuli and expectations, which can lead to feelings of overwhelm and anxiety. By teaching children mindfulness techniques, we can help them learn how to calm their minds and bodies, and cultivate a sense of inner peace and well-being. Research has shown that mindfulness practice can decrease levels of cortisol, the stress hormone, in children, and improve their ability to regulate their emotions.

Furthermore, teaching mindfulness to children can improve their focus and attention span. In a world characterized by distractions and constant stimulation, many children struggle to pay attention and stay focused on a task. By teaching children mindfulness techniques, we can help them develop the capacity to pay attention to the present moment, without being distracted by thoughts or worries. This can lead to improved academic performance, as well as increased creativity and problem-solving skills.

Another important benefit of teaching mindfulness to children is that it can help them develop greater self-awareness and emotional intelligence. Mindfulness practice involves paying attention to one's thoughts, feelings, and bodily sensations with curiosity and kindness. By teaching children mindfulness techniques, we can help them develop a deeper understanding of their own inner world, and cultivate a greater sense of empathy and compassion towards themselves and others. This can lead to stronger interpersonal relationships, as well as a greater sense of self-confidence and self-esteem.

In addition, teaching mindfulness to children can help them develop better coping skills and resilience in the face of adversity. Life is full of ups and downs, and children will inevitably encounter challenges and obstacles along their journey. By teaching children mindfulness techniques, we can help them develop the capacity to respond to difficult situations with calmness and clarity, rather than react impulsively out of fear or anger. This can help children develop a greater sense of resilience, and bounce back more easily from setbacks and disappointments. By teaching children mindfulness techniques, we are equipping them with valuable tools to help them manage stress and anxiety, improve their focus and attention span, develop self-awareness and emotional intelligence, and cultivate greater resilience in the face of adversity. Mindfulness is a lifelong skill that can benefit children well into adulthood, helping them lead happier, healthier, and more fulfilling lives.

- Promoting presence and connection

Promoting presence and connection is a crucial aspect of building strong relationships, whether in professional or personal settings. It involves being fully engaged and attentive in interactions, fostering genuine connections with others, and creating a sense of belonging and trust. By prioritizing presence and connection, individuals can enhance their communication skills, deepen their relationships, and foster a positive and supportive environment.

One key element of promoting presence and connection is active listening. Active listening involves not only hearing what someone is saying but also understanding their perspective, emotions, and intentions. It requires focused attention, empathy, and a genuine interest in what the other person is expressing. By actively listening, individuals can demonstrate respect, validate others' feelings, and build rapport. This can lead to more meaningful and impactful conversations, as well as a stronger sense of connection and understanding between individuals.

Another important aspect of promoting presence and connection is nonverbal communication. Nonverbal cues, such as body language, facial expressions, and tone of voice, can convey powerful messages and emotions that words alone may not capture. By paying attention to nonverbal signals and being mindful of one's own body language, individuals can enhance their communication skills and create a more positive and welcoming environment for others. Nonverbal communication can help to foster trust, empathy, and connection, and can play a crucial role in building strong and meaningful relationships.

In addition to active listening and nonverbal communication, promoting presence and connection also involves being authentic and genuine in interactions. Authenticity is about being true to oneself, expressing one's thoughts and feelings honestly, and staying true to one's values and beliefs. By being authentic, individuals can build trust, credibility, and mutual respect with others, and create a deeper sense of connection and understanding. Authenticity can also help to foster a more positive and supportive environment, where people feel comfortable being themselves and sharing their ideas and opinions openly.

Furthermore, promoting presence and connection requires being mindful of one's own presence and energy in interactions. This involves being present in the moment, focusing on the person or task at hand, and being aware of one's emotions, thoughts, and reactions. By cultivating mindfulness, individuals can improve their self-awareness, emotional intelligence, and ability to regulate their own behavior. This can lead to more effective communication, better decision-making, and a greater sense of connection and empathy with others. Being mindful of one's presence and energy can also help individuals to stay grounded, centered, and focused in interactions, which can enhance their overall presence and impact. By prioritizing active listening, nonverbal communication, authenticity, and mindfulness in interactions, individuals can enhance their communication skills, deepen their relationships with others, and create a more positive and supportive environment. Ultimately, promoting presence and connection can lead to more meaningful conversations, stronger connections, and a greater sense of belonging and trust in relationships. By cultivating these skills and qualities, individuals can become more effective communicators, collaborators, and leaders, and create a more connected and engaged community.

Chapter 13: Navigating Transitions and Challenges

. . . .

- COPING WITH LIFE CHANGES

Life is a journey filled with transitions, challenges, and unexpected changes. Coping with life changes is an essential skill that can help us navigate through the ups and downs of life with resilience and grace. Whether it's starting a new job, moving to a new city, going through a breakup, or experiencing the loss of a loved one, life changes can be overwhelming and stressful. However, with the right mindset and coping strategies, we can adapt to these changes and emerge stronger and more resilient than ever.

One of the key elements of coping with life changes is acceptance. Acceptance involves acknowledging the reality of the situation and letting go of any resistance or denial. It's important to recognize that change is a natural part of life and that resisting it will only lead to more stress and anxiety. By accepting the reality of the situation, we can begin to process our emotions and move forward.

Another crucial aspect of coping with life changes is self-care. Taking care of ourselves physically, mentally, and emotionally is essential during times of transition. This can involve engaging in activities that bring us joy and relaxation, such as exercise, meditation, spending time with loved ones, or engaging in hobbies. Taking care of our physical health through proper nutrition, exercise, and sleep is also important in maintaining our overall well-being during times of change.

In addition to self-care, seeking support from others can be incredibly beneficial when coping with life changes. Whether it's talking to a trusted friend or family member, seeking guidance from a therapist or counselor, or joining a support group, reaching out to others for support can provide us with a sense of connection and reassurance during challenging times. Having a strong support system can help us feel less alone and more capable of navigating through life changes.

Developing coping skills and strategies can also help us better manage the stress and uncertainty that often accompany life changes. This can involve practicing mindfulness and relaxation techniques, such as deep breathing exercises or progressive muscle relaxation. It can also involve reframing negative thoughts and focusing on the positives in our lives, such as gratitude and resilience. Developing coping skills can help us build our resilience and adaptability, allowing us to navigate through life changes with greater ease.

To recapitulate, staying adaptable and open-minded is key when coping with life changes. Being willing to embrace new opportunities, learn from our experiences, and adapt to new circumstances can help us grow and thrive in the face of change. By staying flexible and open to new possibilities, we can approach life changes with a sense of curiosity and optimism, knowing that we have the inner strength and resources to handle whatever comes our way. By embracing change as a natural part of life and approaching it with resilience and grace, we can navigate through life's transitions with strength and confidence. Remember that it's okay to seek help and support when needed, and to be gentle with yourself during times of change. Ultimately, coping with life changes is an opportunity for growth and self-discovery, and a chance to emerge stronger and more resilient than ever before.

- Supporting children through transitions

Supporting children through transitions is a critical aspect of child development and care. Transitions can be defined as any significant changes or moves that children experience in their lives, such as starting school, moving to a new home, or the arrival of a new sibling. These transitions can be challenging for children as they navigate unfamiliar environments, routines, and relationships. It is essential for parents, teachers, and caregivers to understand the impact of transitions on children and provide support to help them adjust and thrive during these periods of change.

One of the key factors in supporting children through transitions is creating a sense of consistency and predictability in their lives. Children thrive on routine and structure, and disruptions to their familiar patterns can lead to feelings of anxiety and insecurity. It is essential for parents and caregivers to establish a routine that provides stability and predictability for children during times of transition. This can include maintaining consistent meal and bedtimes, as well as providing regular opportunities for play, exploration, and relaxation.

In addition to maintaining a sense of routine, it is also crucial for adults to communicate openly and honestly with children about the upcoming transition. Children may feel confused or scared about changes in their lives, and it is essential for adults to validate their feelings and provide reassurance and support. Adults should take the time to explain the reasons for the transition, answer any questions children may have, and involve them in the decision-making process when appropriate. By keeping the lines of communication open, adults can help children feel more secure and confident as they navigate new experiences.

Another important aspect of supporting children through transitions is promoting resilience and problem-solving skills. Transitions can be challenging, but they also present valuable opportunities for children to develop skills such as adaptability, flexibility, and emotional regulation. Adults can help children build these skills by encouraging them to problem-solve, cope with setbacks, and learn from their experiences. By fostering a growth mindset and encouraging children to see transitions as opportunities for growth and learning, adults can help children develop a sense of resilience that will serve them well throughout their lives.

Furthermore, it is essential for adults to provide emotional support and nurturing during times of transition. Children may experience a range of emotions during periods of change, including sadness, anger, fear, and confusion. It is essential for adults to create a safe and supportive environment where children feel comfortable expressing their feelings and seeking comfort when needed. Adults can help children process their emotions by listening attentively, offering empathy and understanding, and providing reassurance that their feelings are normal and valid. By offering emotional support and nurturing, adults can help children feel more secure and confident as they navigate transitions. Transitions can be challenging for children, but with the right support from parents, teachers, and caregivers, children can navigate these changes successfully and thrive. By creating a sense of consistency, communicating openly and honestly, promoting resilience and problem-solving skills, and providing emotional support and nurturing, adults can help children build the skills and confidence they need to face transitions with strength and resilience. Ultimately, by supporting children through transitions, adults can help them grow and thrive as they navigate the many changes and challenges that life presents.

- Dealing with difficult situations

Dealing with difficult situations is a common challenge that we all face at some point in our lives. Whether it be a conflict with a coworker, a disagreement with a loved one, or a personal struggle with anxiety or stress, navigating through tough times requires patience, resilience, and effective problem-solving skills. In this essay, we will explore various strategies and techniques to help individuals cope with difficult situations in a healthy and constructive manner.

One of the first steps in dealing with difficult situations is to acknowledge and accept the fact that challenges are a natural part of life. Rather than avoiding or denying the existence of a problem, it is important to confront it head-on and take proactive steps towards finding a solution. This may involve seeking support from friends, family, or a therapist, and being honest with yourself about your emotions and vulnerabilities. By recognizing and accepting the reality of a difficult situation, you can begin to work towards overcoming it with a clear and focused mindset.

Another key aspect of dealing with difficult situations is practicing self-care and maintaining a positive outlook. It is easy to become overwhelmed and consumed by stress, anxiety, or negative emotions when faced with a challenging circumstance. However, by taking care of your physical, emotional, and mental well-being, you can build resilience and strength to overcome adversity. This may involve engaging in activities that bring you joy and relaxation, such as exercise, mindfulness practices, or hobbies. Additionally, practicing gratitude and focusing on the positive aspects of your life can help shift your perspective and provide a sense of hope and optimism during tough times.

In addition to self-care, effective communication is essential in navigating through difficult situations. Clear and open communication with others can help clarify misunderstandings, address conflicts, and find common ground. It is important to express your thoughts and feelings in a respectful and assertive manner, while also actively listening to the perspectives of others. By engaging in honest and empathetic conversations, you can build trust and strengthen relationships, even in the midst of adversity. Moreover, seeking feedback and guidance from trusted individuals can offer valuable insights and support in finding solutions to complex problems.

Furthermore, developing problem-solving skills and resilience can empower individuals to overcome challenges and obstacles with confidence and courage. Instead of giving in to feelings of helplessness or despair, it is important to approach difficult situations with a sense of determination and perseverance. This may involve breaking down the problem into smaller, manageable steps, setting realistic goals, and creating action plans to address each issue systematically. By staying focused and proactive in your approach, you can increase your capacity to handle tough situations and adapt to changing circumstances with resilience and grace.

Lastly, learning from difficult situations and growing from adversity can lead to personal growth and development. Every challenge and setback presents an opportunity for self-reflection, learning, and improvement. By reflecting on the lessons learned from past experiences, you can gain valuable insights into your strengths, weaknesses, and areas for growth. This self-awareness can help you develop the skills and qualities needed to cope with future difficulties in a more effective and proactive manner. Ultimately, by embracing challenges and using them as opportunities for personal growth and learning, you can build resilience, confidence, and a sense of empowerment to navigate through life's ups and downs with grace and resilience. By acknowledging the reality of a problem, practicing self-care, communicating effectively, developing problem-solving skills, and learning from adversity, individuals can navigate through tough times with resilience and grace. While it may be challenging and uncomfortable to confront difficult situations, it is through perseverance and personal growth that we can overcome obstacles and thrive in the face of adversity. By embracing challenges as opportunities for growth and empowerment, we can cultivate resilience, build meaningful relationships, and lead fulfilling lives despite life's inevitable ups and downs.

Chapter 14: Promoting Mental Health and Well-being

....

- RECOGNIZING SIGNS of mental health issues

Mental health issues are a pervasive and often misunderstood aspect of human health. Recognizing the signs of mental health issues is crucial in order to provide appropriate support and intervention for those in need. In today's society, there is a growing awareness and destigmatization of mental health concerns, making it more important than ever to be able to identify and address potential problems in ourselves and others.

One common misconception about mental health is that it only affects a certain subset of individuals, such as those with a diagnosed mental illness. In reality, mental health is a spectrum that fluctuates for everyone. Just as physical health can vary from day to day, so too can mental health. It is important to recognize that mental health issues can affect anyone, regardless of age, gender, or background. This is why it is crucial to be able to identify the signs of mental health issues in ourselves and in those around us.

There are many signs and symptoms that may indicate a mental health issue. These can manifest differently depending on the individual and the specific condition they are experiencing. Some common signs of mental health issues include changes in mood, behavior, and cognition. For example, someone who is typically outgoing and social may become withdrawn and isolated, indicating possible depression or anxiety. Likewise, drastic changes in eating or sleeping patterns, as well as difficulty concentrating or making decisions, may be signs of a mental health issue.

Another important aspect of recognizing signs of mental health issues is understanding the stigma that surrounds mental illness. Many people are hesitant to seek help for mental health concerns due to fear of judgment or discrimination. This stigma can prevent individuals from getting the support they need and contribute to the worsening of their symptoms. By being aware of the stigma surrounding mental health, we can work to create a more supportive and understanding environment that encourages open discussion and destigmatization.

It is also important to remember that mental health issues are complex and multifaceted. They can be influenced by a variety of factors, including genetics, environment, and life experiences. This means that there is not a one-size-fits-all approach to identifying and addressing mental health concerns. It is crucial to take a holistic view of mental health and consider all aspects of an individual's life when assessing their mental well-being.

In order to effectively recognize signs of mental health issues, it is important to educate yourself on the topic. There are a variety of resources available, including online articles, books, and workshops, that can provide valuable information and guidance on how to identify and address mental health concerns. Additionally, seeking out professional help from a therapist, counselor, or mental health professional can provide expert insight and support in navigating mental health issues. By understanding the complexities of mental health, recognizing common signs and symptoms, and addressing the stigma surrounding mental illness, we can create a more compassionate and supportive society that prioritizes mental well-being. It is important to prioritize mental health awareness and education in order to ensure that everyone has the resources and support they need to thrive.

- Supporting emotional well-being

Emotional well-being refers to the ability to effectively manage and navigate one's emotions, as well as maintain a positive outlook on life. It encompasses emotional regulation, resilience, self-awareness, and the ability to cope with stress and difficult situations.

There are various ways to support emotional well-being, and it is important to understand that each person's needs and preferences are unique. One key aspect of supporting emotional well-being is self-care. Self-care encompasses activities that help individuals to relax, de-stress, and rejuvenate themselves. This can include activities such as exercise, meditation, journaling, spending time in nature, or engaging in hobbies and interests. Taking the time to prioritize self-care can help individuals to better manage their emotions and maintain a healthy emotional balance.

Another important aspect of supporting emotional well-being is developing healthy coping mechanisms. Coping mechanisms are strategies individuals use to manage stress, emotions, and difficult situations. Healthy coping mechanisms can include activities such as talking to a trusted friend or counselor, practicing mindfulness, engaging in creative outlets, or engaging in physical activity. By developing healthy coping mechanisms, individuals can build resilience and better navigate the ups and downs of life.

In addition to self-care and healthy coping mechanisms, social support is also crucial in supporting emotional well-being. Social support refers to having a network of friends, family, and other individuals who provide emotional support, guidance, and companionship. This can include having someone to talk to when you're feeling overwhelmed, having someone to lean on during difficult times, or simply having someone who can provide a listening ear. Social support can help individuals feel connected, valued, and understood, which can have a positive impact on their emotional well-being.

It is also important to recognize the role that mental health professionals play in supporting emotional well-being. Therapists, counselors, and other mental health professionals can provide individuals with tools, strategies, and support to help them navigate their emotions, cope with stress, and address underlying issues that may be impacting their emotional well-being. Seeking professional help is not a sign of weakness, but rather a proactive step towards prioritizing one's emotional health and well-being. Remember, it is okay to ask for help and to prioritize your emotional well-being – you deserve to live a happy and fulfilling life.

- Seeking professional help when needed

Seeking professional help when needed is a crucial step in maintaining our mental and emotional well-being. While there may be a stigma surrounding therapy and counseling, it is important to recognize that seeking help is a sign of strength and self-awareness. In today's fast-paced and demanding world, it is easy to become overwhelmed and feel like we are struggling to cope with our emotions and stressors. This is where professional help can make a significant difference in our lives.

Therapy and counseling provide a safe and non-judgmental space for individuals to explore their thoughts, feelings, and behaviors. A trained therapist or counselor can offer valuable insights, perspectives, and coping strategies to help navigate through life's challenges. Whether it is dealing with relationship issues, managing anxiety or depression, or coping with trauma, therapy can provide the support and guidance needed to heal and grow.

It is important to recognize that seeking professional help is not a sign of weakness, but rather a proactive step towards self-improvement and personal growth. Just as we seek out medical help when we are physically unwell, it is equally important to seek out mental health support when we are struggling emotionally. Mental health is just as important as physical health, and investing in our well-being should be a top priority.

In addition to individual therapy, group therapy and support groups can also be beneficial for those who are looking for peer support and a sense of community. Group therapy provides a safe space to share experiences, receive feedback, and build connections with others who are facing similar challenges. It can be comforting to know that we are not alone in our struggles and to gain insight and perspective from others who are on a similar journey.

When considering seeking professional help, it is important to find a therapist or counselor who is a good fit for your needs and preferences. It may take some time to find the right match, but it is worth the effort to find someone who makes you feel comfortable, understood, and supported. Therapists and counselors come from diverse backgrounds and specialties, so it is important to do some research and ask for recommendations to find the best fit for you.

In addition to therapy and counseling, there are a variety of other resources and support systems available for those in need. This may include online therapy platforms, support hotlines, crisis intervention services, and community mental health centers. It is important to reach out and ask for help when needed, as there are professionals and organizations dedicated to providing support and assistance to those in need.

Ultimately, seeking professional help when needed is a courageous and empowering choice that can lead to personal growth, healing, and resilience. It is important to prioritize your mental health and well-being, and to recognize that you deserve to feel supported and cared for. By taking the step to seek help, you are investing in yourself and your future, and opening yourself up to the possibility of positive change and transformation. Remember that you are not alone in your struggles, and that there is help and support available to guide you on your journey towards healing and well-being.

Chapter 15: Encouraging Physical Health

. . . .

- PROMOTING HEALTHY habits

Promoting healthy habits is essential for maintaining overall well-being and preventing chronic diseases. Healthy habits encompass a range of practices that contribute to physical, mental, and emotional health. These habits include regular exercise, balanced nutrition, adequate sleep, stress management, and avoidance of harmful substances such as tobacco and excessive alcohol. By incorporating these habits into our daily routine, we can improve our quality of life and reduce the risk of developing conditions such as obesity, heart disease, diabetes, and depression.

One of the most effective ways to promote healthy habits is through education and awareness. By providing individuals with accurate information about the benefits of healthy habits and the risks of unhealthy behaviors, we can empower them to make informed choices about their health. This can be done through educational campaigns, workshops, and seminars that focus on topics such as nutrition, exercise, and stress management. By emphasizing the importance of taking care of our bodies and minds, we can motivate people to prioritize their health and make positive changes in their lifestyle.

In addition to education, it is important to create environments that support healthy habits. This can involve making healthy options more accessible and affordable, such as by providing nutritious food choices in school cafeterias, workplaces, and public spaces. It can also involve implementing policies that encourage physical activity, such as building bike lanes or creating walking paths in communities. By making healthy choices the easy choice, we can help individuals adopt and maintain habits that contribute to their overall well-being.

Another key aspect of promoting healthy habits is fostering social support and accountability. Studies have shown that people are more likely to stick to their health goals when they have the support of friends, family, or community members. This can involve setting goals together, exercising with a buddy, or joining a support group for weight loss or smoking cessation. By surrounding ourselves with like-minded individuals who share our commitment to health, we can stay motivated and accountable in our efforts to maintain healthy habits.

It is also important to recognize that healthy habits are not one-size-fits-all. Each individual is unique, with their own preferences, needs, and challenges when it comes to adopting healthy behaviors. Therefore, promoting healthy habits should be personalized and tailored to each person's specific circumstances. This may involve working with a healthcare provider or dietitian to create a customized nutrition plan, or seeking the guidance of a personal trainer to design an exercise program that is suitable for one's fitness level and goals. By taking into account individual differences and preferences, we can help people find sustainable and enjoyable ways to incorporate healthy habits into their daily life.

Ultimately, promoting healthy habits is a collective effort that requires collaboration between individuals, communities, healthcare providers, policymakers, and businesses. By working together to create a culture of health and wellness, we can empower people to take control of their health and make positive choices that will benefit them in the long run. By emphasizing the importance of prevention and proactive self-care, we can reduce the burden of chronic disease and create a healthier and happier society for all.

- Encouraging physical activity

Encouraging physical activity is crucial for maintaining a healthy lifestyle and preventing various chronic diseases. Research has shown that regular physical activity can improve cardiovascular health, increase muscle strength, enhance flexibility, and boost overall well-being. However, despite the numerous benefits of staying active, many individuals struggle to incorporate regular exercise into their daily routines. This can be due to a variety of factors, such as lack of time, motivation, or knowledge about exercise options.

One of the key strategies for encouraging physical activity is to make it enjoyable and accessible. It's important to find an activity that you enjoy and that fits your personality and lifestyle. This could be anything from taking a dance class, going for a brisk walk in the park, or playing a sport with friends. By choosing an activity that you find enjoyable, you are more likely to stick with it in the long term. Additionally, finding a physical activity that fits into your schedule and can be easily incorporated into your daily routine can help make exercise a habit.

Another important factor in encouraging physical activity is setting realistic goals and tracking your progress. By setting specific, measurable, achievable, relevant, and time-bound (SMART) goals, you can stay motivated and focused on your fitness journey. Whether your goal is to lose weight, improve your cardiovascular fitness, or simply increase your daily step count, having a clear objective can help you stay on track and see progress over time. Using a fitness tracker or journal to record your workouts and activity levels can also help you stay accountable and motivated to continue exercising.

In addition to setting goals, it's important to vary your physical activities to prevent boredom and keep your body challenged. Mixing up your routine with different types of exercise, such as cardio, strength training, flexibility exercises, and mind-body practices like yoga or tai chi, can help you avoid plateaus and continue making progress towards your fitness goals. This variety can also help prevent injuries and overuse of certain muscle groups, as well as keep you engaged and excited about your workouts.

Social support is another key aspect of encouraging physical activity. Exercising with friends, family members, or in a group setting can provide motivation, accountability, and a sense of community that can make the experience more enjoyable and rewarding. Whether you join a fitness class, start a walking group with coworkers, or participate in team sports, having others to exercise with can help you stay committed to your fitness goals and provide an opportunity for social interaction and connection. Encouraging physical activity in a social context can also make it more fun and engaging, as you may be more likely to push yourself and try new activities with the encouragement and support of others.

Incorporating physical activity into your daily life can also be as simple as making small changes to your routine. Taking the stairs instead of the elevator, parking further away from the entrance, walking or biking to work, or doing household chores like gardening or cleaning can all add up to increased physical activity throughout the day. Finding opportunities to move more during your daily activities can help you stay active and maintain a healthy lifestyle without having to dedicate large blocks of time specifically for exercise. Additionally, incorporating physical activity into your daily routine can help you build consistency and make exercise a natural part of your lifestyle. By finding enjoyable and accessible activities, setting realistic goals, tracking progress, varying your workout routine, seeking social support, and incorporating movement into your daily life, you can create a sustainable fitness plan that fits your lifestyle and helps you achieve your health and fitness goals. Remember that any amount of physical activity is better than none, so start small, stay consistent, and celebrate your progress along the way. By making exercise a priority and a positive part of your daily routine, you can improve your physical and mental health, boost your energy levels, and enhance your quality of life.

- Teaching the importance of self-care

Self-care is an essential aspect of overall well-being and mental health that is often overlooked or neglected in today's fast-paced society. In order to live a healthy and fulfilling life, it is important to prioritize self-care practices and make them a regular part of our daily routines. Teaching the importance of self-care to individuals of all ages is crucial in promoting self-awareness, resilience, and emotional regulation. By understanding the significance of self-care and implementing effective strategies, individuals can better manage stress, improve their mental health, and enhance their overall quality of life.

One of the key principles of self-care is the idea that taking care of oneself is not selfish, but rather necessary for optimal functioning and well-being. It is important for individuals to recognize that self-care is not a luxury, but a fundamental aspect of maintaining physical, emotional, and mental health. By prioritizing self-care activities, individuals can prevent burnout, reduce stress, and cultivate a sense of balance and well-being in their lives. Teaching individuals the importance of self-care involves challenging the notion that self-sacrifice and self-neglect are noble or virtuous behaviors. Instead, it is important to promote the idea that self-care is essential for maintaining a healthy relationship with oneself and enhancing overall quality of life.

In order to effectively teach the importance of self-care, it is essential to first understand what self-care entails and the various forms it can take. Self-care involves engaging in activities that promote physical, emotional, and mental well-being, such as exercise, mindfulness, relaxation, and social connection. It is important for individuals to identify their own unique self-care needs and preferences, and to explore different strategies and techniques that work best for them. By encouraging individuals to prioritize self-care activities that resonate with them personally, teachers and educators can help individuals develop a sustainable and effective self-care routine that fits their individual needs and lifestyles.

Teaching the importance of self-care also involves emphasizing the importance of self-awareness and mindfulness in promoting overall well-being. By encouraging individuals to cultivate self-awareness and pay attention to their thoughts, feelings, and behaviors, educators can help individuals identify early warning signs of stress, anxiety, and burnout. By teaching individuals how to practice mindfulness and self-reflection, educators can empower individuals to make conscious choices about their self-care practices and take proactive steps to maintain their physical, emotional, and mental health. By promoting self-awareness and mindfulness in the context of self-care, educators can help individuals develop a deeper understanding of themselves and their needs, and cultivate a sense of resilience and emotional regulation in the face of life's challenges.

In addition to promoting self-awareness and mindfulness, teaching the importance of self-care also involves educating individuals about the impact of lifestyle factors on mental health and well-being. It is important for individuals to understand how factors such as sleep, nutrition, exercise, and social connection can impact their mental health and overall quality of life. By teaching individuals about the importance of maintaining a healthy lifestyle, educators can empower individuals to make informed choices about their self-care practices and create a supportive environment for their well-being. By promoting the connection between lifestyle choices and mental health, educators can help individuals take a holistic approach to self-care and promote overall well-being in all areas of their lives.

Another important aspect of teaching the importance of self-care is promoting the value of self-compassion and self-acceptance in the self-care process. It is important for individuals to cultivate a sense of self-compassion and self-acceptance in order to promote emotional well-being and resilience. By encouraging individuals to practice self-compassion and to treat themselves with kindness and understanding, educators can help individuals build a positive relationship with themselves and foster a sense of self-worth and self-esteem. By promoting self-compassion in the context of self-care, educators can help individuals develop a sense of resilience and emotional strength in the face of adversity and challenges. By emphasizing the importance of self-compassion and self-acceptance in the self-care process, educators can help individuals create a supportive and nurturing environment for their well-being and promote a sense of balance and inner peace in their lives. By promoting self-awareness, mindfulness, healthy lifestyle choices, and self-compassion in the context of self-care, educators can empower individuals to take an active role in maintaining their physical, emotional, and mental health. By teaching individuals the importance of self-care and providing them with the necessary tools and strategies to prioritize their well-being, educators can help individuals cultivate a sense of balance, resilience, and emotional regulation in their lives. By promoting the value of self-care and self-compassion in the self-care process, educators can help individuals create a supportive and nurturing environment for their well-being and promote a sense of inner peace and well-being in their lives.

Chapter 16: Supporting Educational Success

• • • •

- PARTNERING WITH SCHOOLS and teachers

Partnering with schools and teachers is a crucial aspect of promoting education and fostering academic success in students. Collaborating with educators allows for a more holistic approach to supporting students, as teachers are on the front lines of education and have a deep understanding of their students' needs and strengths. By working together with schools and teachers, organizations can enhance the learning experience for students, provide valuable resources and support to educators, and create a strong community of stakeholders invested in the success of students.

One of the key benefits of partnering with schools and teachers is the opportunity to align resources and efforts to support student learning. Schools are often faced with limited budgets and resources, which can make it challenging to provide students with the tools and opportunities they need to succeed academically. By partnering with external organizations, schools can access additional resources, expertise, and support to supplement their existing programs and initiatives. This can include providing funding for educational materials, technology, or extracurricular activities, as well as offering professional development opportunities for teachers to enhance their skills and knowledge.

Furthermore, partnering with schools and teachers can help organizations better understand and address the unique needs of students in different communities. Teachers have a wealth of knowledge about their students' backgrounds, interests, and learning styles, which can inform the development of more targeted and effective programs and services. By collaborating with educators, organizations can gain insights into the specific challenges and opportunities facing students in a particular school or district, and tailor their efforts to meet the needs of those students. This personalized approach to supporting student learning can lead to better outcomes and greater impact in the long run.

In addition to enhancing student learning, partnering with schools and teachers can also benefit educators by providing them with valuable resources, support, and opportunities for professional growth. Teachers are often overworked and under-resourced, with limited time and funding to pursue professional development or access the latest teaching tools and techniques. By partnering with external organizations, teachers can benefit from additional training, mentoring, and resources to help them improve their teaching practices and better support their students. This can lead to increased job satisfaction, retention, and effectiveness among educators, ultimately benefiting students and the broader education community.

Moreover, partnering with schools and teachers can help organizations build a strong community of stakeholders invested in the success of students. Education is a collective effort that requires the collaboration and support of teachers, parents, administrators, and other stakeholders to create a positive and enriching learning environment for students. By engaging with schools and teachers, organizations can foster strong relationships with key stakeholders in the education sector, build trust and credibility within the community, and create a sense of shared purpose and commitment to student success. This collaborative approach to education can lead to greater buy-in, support, and participation from all members of the school community, ultimately benefiting students and improving educational outcomes. By collaborating with educators, organizations can enhance student learning, support teachers, address the unique needs of students, and build a strong community of stakeholders invested in the success of students. This collaborative approach to education can lead to better outcomes, increased engagement, and greater impact in the long run. By working together with schools and teachers, organizations can create a more inclusive, supportive, and effective learning environment that benefits all members of the education community.

- Advocating for your child's education

Advocating for your child's education is a crucial aspect of parenting that goes beyond simply ensuring their attendance in school. It involves actively engaging with teachers, administrators, and other stakeholders to ensure that your child receives the best possible education and support. Advocacy can take many forms, from attending parent-teacher conferences and volunteering at your child's school to participating in advocacy organizations and lobbying for policy changes at the local or state level.

One of the key reasons why advocating for your child's education is so important is because it helps to ensure that they receive a high-quality education that meets their individual needs. Every child is unique, with their own strengths, weaknesses, and learning styles. By advocating for your child, you can help to ensure that their educational experience is tailored to their specific needs and abilities, rather than following a one-size-fits-all approach.

Advocating for your child's education also helps to create a positive and supportive learning environment for them. When parents are actively involved in their child's education, it sends a powerful message that education is important and valued. This can have a significant impact on a child's motivation, engagement, and overall academic success. Additionally, when parents advocate for their child, they can help to address any challenges or obstacles that may arise, whether they be academic, social, emotional, or behavioral in nature.

Another important reason to advocate for your child's education is that it can help to promote equity and fairness in the educational system. Unfortunately, not all children have access to the same opportunities and resources when it comes to education. By advocating for your child, you can help to ensure that they have access to the support and opportunities they need to thrive academically. Additionally, by advocating for your child, you can help to identify and address any disparities or inequities that may exist within the educational system, whether they be related to funding, resources, staffing, or curriculum.

There are many ways that parents can advocate for their child's education. One of the most important ways is to establish a positive and open line of communication with your child's teachers and school administrators. This can involve attending parent-teacher conferences, staying informed about your child's progress and needs, and reaching out to teachers and administrators with any questions or concerns you may have. By building strong relationships with your child's educators, you can work together to support your child's academic and personal development.

Another important way to advocate for your child's education is to stay informed about educational policies and practices at the local, state, and national levels. This can involve staying up-to-date on changes in curriculum, assessments, standards, and other educational policies that may impact your child's education. By staying informed, you can be better equipped to advocate for policies and practices that will benefit your child and other students in the long run.

In addition to staying informed and building relationships with your child's educators, parents can also advocate for their child by getting involved in advocacy organizations and campaigns. There are many organizations at the local, state, and national levels that work to improve educational opportunities and outcomes for all students. By joining one of these organizations, parents can work together with other advocates to push for positive changes in the educational system. This can involve everything from lobbying for increased funding for schools to advocating for policies that support parent and community involvement in education.

Ultimately, advocating for your child's education is a powerful way to support their growth, development, and success. By actively engaging with teachers, administrators, and other stakeholders, parents can help to ensure that their child receives a high-quality education that meets their individual needs. Advocacy can take many forms, from building relationships with educators and staying informed about educational policies to getting involved in advocacy organizations and campaigns. By advocating for your child's education, you can help to create a positive and supportive learning environment, promote equity and fairness in the educational system, and collaborate with others to improve educational opportunities and outcomes for all students.

- Setting academic goals and expectations

Setting academic goals and expectations is a crucial step in ensuring success in your academic journey. By clearly defining what you want to achieve and the standards you hold yourself to, you can create a roadmap for your education and stay motivated throughout the process. When setting academic goals, it's important to be specific, measurable, achievable, relevant, and time-bound. This is known as the SMART criteria, and it can help you create goals that are clear and actionable.

One of the first steps in setting academic goals is to reflect on your strengths and weaknesses, as well as your long-term objectives. By understanding where you excel and where you need improvement, you can tailor your goals to address these areas. It's also important to consider your long-term career aspirations and how your academic goals align with them. For example, if you want to pursue a career in medicine, your academic goals may revolve around maintaining a high GPA, gaining research experience, and excelling in science courses.

Another important aspect of setting academic goals is to break them down into smaller, more manageable tasks. This can help prevent overwhelm and allow you to track your progress more effectively. For example, if your goal is to improve your writing skills, you could break it down into tasks such as reading academic articles, practicing writing essays, and seeking feedback from professors. By breaking your goals into smaller steps, you can stay focused and make steady progress towards your ultimate objective.

In addition to setting specific academic goals, it's also important to establish expectations for yourself. This includes the standards of quality you hold yourself to, as well as the behaviors and habits you expect to exhibit. For example, you may expect yourself to attend all classes, actively participate in discussions, and turn in assignments on time. By setting clear expectations for yourself, you can hold yourself accountable and maintain a high level of performance in your academic endeavors.

It's also important to be flexible with your academic goals and expectations, as unforeseen circumstances may arise that can impact your progress. For example, if you encounter a personal or health-related issue that affects your ability to meet your goals, it's important to adjust your expectations and goals accordingly. Being able to adapt to changing circumstances is a key skill in navigating the academic landscape and achieving success. By following the SMART criteria, reflecting on your strengths and weaknesses, breaking down goals into smaller tasks, and establishing clear expectations for yourself, you can create a roadmap for your education that is tailored to your unique strengths and aspirations. By maintaining flexibility and adaptability, you can navigate challenges and setbacks with resilience and ultimately achieve your academic goals.

Chapter 17: Cultivating Creativity and Imagination

• • • •

- FOSTERING CREATIVE expression

Fostering creative expression is a critical aspect of human development and overall well-being. Creativity is not just about artistic endeavors; it encompasses problem-solving skills, innovative thinking, and the ability to adapt to new situations. By nurturing creativity in individuals, we empower them to think outside the box, explore new ideas, and express themselves in unique ways. Creative expression can lead to greater self-awareness, improved mental health, and enhanced communication skills.

One way to foster creative expression is to provide a supportive and encouraging environment. This can be achieved through open communication, constructive feedback, and opportunities for collaboration. When individuals feel valued and supported in their creative endeavors, they are more likely to take risks, try new things, and push boundaries. By creating a culture that celebrates creativity and rewards experimentation, we can inspire individuals to explore their creative potential and unleash their imagination.

Another important aspect of fostering creative expression is providing access to resources and tools that support creative pursuits. This includes providing access to art supplies, technology, and other resources that enable individuals to explore different mediums and techniques. By removing barriers to creativity and providing the necessary tools and resources, we can empower individuals to express themselves in new and innovative ways. Additionally, providing training and education in creative skills can help individuals develop their artistic abilities and expand their creative capabilities.

In order to foster creative expression, it is important to encourage interdisciplinary collaboration and cross-pollination of ideas. By bringing together individuals from diverse backgrounds and disciplines, we can spark creativity and innovation. Collaborating with others allows for the exchange of ideas, perspectives, and experiences, leading to the development of unique and innovative solutions. By fostering a collaborative environment that values diversity and inclusivity, we can create a fertile ground for creative expression to flourish.

In addition to providing support, resources, and opportunities for collaboration, it is also important to nurture a growth mindset in individuals. A growth mindset is the belief that intelligence and abilities can be developed through hard work, dedication, and learning from failure. By cultivating a growth mindset in individuals, we can inspire them to embrace challenges, persist in the face of adversity, and continually seek opportunities for growth and improvement. This mindset is essential for fostering creative expression, as it encourages individuals to take risks, learn from mistakes, and continuously push themselves to explore new avenues of creativity.

Ultimately, fostering creative expression is about creating an environment that empowers individuals to tap into their innate creativity and express themselves in meaningful ways. By providing support, resources, opportunities for collaboration, and nurturing a growth mindset, we can inspire individuals to unleash their creative potential and make a positive impact on the world around them. In doing so, we can foster a culture of creativity, innovation, and imagination that benefits not only individuals but society as a whole.

- Encouraging imagination and play

Encouraging imagination and play in children is essential for their overall development and well-being. Imagination is the ability to create mental images, ideas, and scenarios that are not present in reality. It allows children to think creatively, problem-solve, and explore new possibilities. Play, on the other hand, is a natural means through which children learn about the world around them, develop social skills, and build emotional resilience. When children engage in imaginative play, they are not only having fun, but they are also enhancing their cognitive, emotional, and social abilities.

One way to encourage imagination and play in children is to provide them with open-ended toys and materials that allow for creative exploration. Toys like building blocks, art supplies, and dress-up clothes can inspire children to use their imagination and engage in imaginative play. These types of toys do not have a predetermined outcome, allowing children to come up with their own scenarios and storylines. By stimulating their creativity in this way, children can learn to think outside the box, problem-solve, and develop their own unique ideas.

Another way to encourage imagination and play in children is to create a supportive environment that fosters creativity and exploration. Parents and caregivers can set aside time and space for children to engage in imaginative play, whether that means turning off screens and electronics, setting up a play area with toys and materials, or joining in on the play themselves. By actively participating in their children's imaginative play, adults can help to foster creativity, reinforce positive social interactions, and strengthen the parent-child bond.

In addition to providing open-ended toys and creating a supportive environment, adults can also encourage imagination and play in children by modeling creativity and playfulness themselves. When children see adults engaging in imaginative activities, such as storytelling, drawing, or playing make-believe games, they are more likely to feel inspired to do the same. By demonstrating a playful and imaginative attitude, adults can help to cultivate a culture of creativity and exploration in the home or classroom.

It is important to recognize that imagination and play are not just frivolous activities, but crucial components of a child's development. Research has shown that imaginative play can have numerous benefits for children, including improved cognitive skills, emotional regulation, and social competence. By encouraging children to engage in imaginative play, caregivers and educators are helping to support their overall well-being and development. By providing open-ended toys, creating a supportive environment, and modeling creativity and playfulness, adults can help children to develop their cognitive, emotional, and social abilities. Imagination and play are not only fun activities, but also important tools for learning, problem-solving, and self-expression. By fostering a culture of creativity and exploration, caregivers and educators can help to nurture the imaginations of children and prepare them for success in school and in life.

- Supporting artistic pursuits

Artistic pursuits are a valuable and important aspect of human creativity and expression. From painting and sculpture to music and writing, art plays a crucial role in our lives and society. However, artists often face challenges in pursuing their passions, such as financial constraints, lack of resources, and limited opportunities for exposure. It is essential to support and encourage artists in their creative endeavors to ensure that their talents thrive and contribute to the cultural enrichment of our communities.

One way to support artistic pursuits is through providing funding and grants. Many artists struggle to make a living from their work, and financial support can make a significant difference in their ability to create art. Government agencies, non-profit organizations, and private foundations offer grants and scholarships to artists in various disciplines, allowing them to focus on their craft without the worry of financial instability. By investing in the arts, we are not only supporting individual artists but also fostering a vibrant and diverse cultural landscape.

In addition to financial support, artists also benefit from access to resources and facilities that enhance their creative processes. Studios, workshops, and performance spaces are essential for artists to experiment, collaborate, and present their work to the public. Providing affordable or subsidized access to these resources can help artists develop their skills and build their portfolios. Furthermore, mentorship programs and artist residencies offer valuable guidance and support for emerging artists, facilitating their growth and professional development.

Promoting public engagement with the arts is another crucial aspect of supporting artistic pursuits. Community events, exhibitions, and performances bring artists and audiences together, creating opportunities for dialogue and appreciation of creative work. By participating in or attending these events, individuals can show their support for local artists and contribute to the vitality of their communities. Public art projects, such as murals and installations, also beautify urban spaces and foster a sense of belonging and cultural identity.

Educational initiatives play a significant role in nurturing artistic talent and fostering a culture of creativity. Schools, colleges, and universities offer programs in the arts that not only teach technical skills but also cultivate critical thinking, problem-solving, and communication abilities. By investing in arts education, we are preparing the next generation of artists and creatives to make meaningful contributions to society. Additionally, arts advocacy organizations work to promote the value of arts education and support policies that prioritize the arts in school curricula. By providing financial assistance, access to resources, promoting public engagement, and investing in arts education, we can ensure that artists have the support they need to thrive and contribute to the cultural enrichment of society. Artistic expression is a fundamental aspect of the human experience, and by supporting artists in their creative endeavors, we are fostering a more vibrant and inclusive cultural landscape for all to enjoy.

Chapter 18: Instilling Values and Ethics

• • • •

- TEACHING MORAL VALUES and ethics

Teaching moral values and ethics is a crucial aspect of education that plays a significant role in shaping the character and behavior of individuals. Moral values are the principles that guide a person's decisions and actions, while ethics refer to the societal standards of right and wrong behavior. By teaching moral values and ethics, educators help students develop a strong moral compass and make informed decisions that are rooted in principles of integrity and respect.

One of the key reasons why teaching moral values and ethics is essential is because it helps students understand the importance of integrity and honesty in their interactions with others. In today's fast-paced and competitive world, it is easy for individuals to prioritize success and achievement over ethical considerations. By instilling moral values such as honesty, fairness, and respect in students, educators equip them with the tools to navigate ethical dilemmas and make ethical decisions in their personal and professional lives.

Furthermore, teaching moral values and ethics helps students develop empathy and compassion towards others. In a world that is increasingly diverse and interconnected, it is essential for individuals to understand and appreciate the perspectives and experiences of others. By teaching students the importance of compassion, kindness, and empathy, educators foster a sense of understanding and tolerance among students, leading to a more inclusive and harmonious society.

Moreover, teaching moral values and ethics helps students become responsible citizens who contribute positively to their communities and society at large. By instilling values such as social responsibility, civic engagement, and environmental stewardship, educators empower students to make a difference in the world and advocate for social justice and equity. Through service-learning projects, community service initiatives, and advocacy campaigns, students can apply their moral values and ethics in practical ways that have a meaningful impact on their communities.

In addition, teaching moral values and ethics equips students with the skills and qualities needed to navigate complex ethical dilemmas and make ethical decisions in their personal and professional lives. By promoting critical thinking, moral reasoning, and ethical reflection, educators help students develop the ability to analyze ethical issues, weigh conflicting values, and make sound moral judgments. These skills are essential for individuals to navigate the complexities of the modern world and make ethical decisions that are based on principles of justice, integrity, and compassion.

Moreover, teaching moral values and ethics fosters a culture of ethical leadership and ethical decision-making in schools and organizations. By promoting ethical values such as honesty, integrity, and fairness, educators set a positive example for students and create a climate of trust, respect, and accountability. This, in turn, helps students develop the skills and qualities to be ethical leaders who inspire others, uphold ethical standards, and make principled decisions that benefit the common good. By instilling moral values such as honesty, fairness, and empathy, educators empower students to become responsible citizens who contribute positively to their communities and society at large. Through critical thinking, moral reasoning, and ethical reflection, students can develop the ability to analyze ethical dilemmas, weigh conflicting values, and make sound moral judgments. Ultimately, teaching moral values and ethics fosters a culture of ethical leadership and ethical decision-making that benefits individuals, communities, and society as a whole.

- Modeling integrity and honesty

Integrity and honesty are two essential attributes that play a crucial role in the success of individuals and organizations. Modeling integrity and honesty is not only important for ethical reasons but also for building trust, credibility, and respect. In this essay, we will delve into the significance of integrity and honesty, examine how they can be modeled effectively, and explore the benefits of doing so.

Integrity is often defined as the quality of being honest and having strong moral principles. It involves consistency in thoughts, words, and actions, as well as doing the right thing even when no one is watching. Honesty, on the other hand, refers to truthfulness, transparency, and sincerity in communication. Both integrity and honesty are integral components of ethical behavior and are essential in maintaining trust and credibility in personal and professional relationships.

Modeling integrity and honesty is not just about following a set of rules or guidelines; it is about embodying these qualities in every aspect of one's life. This requires a deep commitment to ethical values and a genuine desire to act with integrity and honesty in all circumstances. It involves being truthful and transparent in one's interactions, taking responsibility for one's actions, and upholding moral principles even in the face of adversity.

One of the most effective ways to model integrity and honesty is through leading by example. People are more likely to emulate behaviors that they see in others, especially those in positions of authority or influence. By demonstrating integrity and honesty in their actions and decisions, leaders can inspire and motivate others to do the same. This can create a culture of accountability and ethical behavior within an organization, leading to increased trust, loyalty, and respect among employees and stakeholders.

Another important aspect of modeling integrity and honesty is maintaining consistency in one's actions and values. It is not enough to talk about integrity and honesty; one must also demonstrate these qualities consistently in all aspects of their life. This means aligning one's words with their actions, being transparent and truthful in all communications, and upholding moral principles even in difficult situations. Consistency is key in building trust and credibility, as people are more likely to trust and respect those who consistently act with integrity and honesty.

In addition to leading by example and maintaining consistency, it is also important to hold oneself accountable for one's actions and decisions. This means taking responsibility for one's mistakes, admitting when one has acted inappropriately, and making amends when necessary. Holding oneself accountable demonstrates a commitment to integrity and honesty and shows others that one is willing to stand by their values even when it is difficult to do so.

Modeling integrity and honesty can have numerous benefits, both on a personal and professional level. In personal relationships, integrity and honesty can help build trust, respect, and strong connections with others. People are more likely to confide in and rely on those who they perceive as honest and trustworthy, leading to deeper and more meaningful relationships.

In the professional realm, integrity and honesty are essential for building a positive reputation, attracting clients and customers, and fostering a positive work culture. Organizations that prioritize integrity and honesty are more likely to gain the trust and loyalty of their employees, customers, and stakeholders, leading to increased productivity, profitability, and sustainability. Moreover, modeling integrity and honesty can help prevent conflicts, misunderstandings, and unethical behaviors within an organization, leading to a more harmonious and productive work environment. By leading by example, maintaining consistency, and holding oneself accountable, individuals can cultivate a culture of integrity and honesty that fosters trust, respect, and credibility. The benefits of modeling integrity and honesty are numerous, ranging from stronger relationships and personal fulfillment to increased trust and loyalty in professional settings. By prioritizing integrity and honesty in all aspects of life, individuals can create a positive impact on themselves and those around them, contributing to a more ethical and transparent society as a whole.

- Promoting social responsibility

Promoting social responsibility is essential in today's society as it encompasses the ethical obligations that individuals and organizations have towards the well-being of the community and the environment. Social responsibility entails conducting business activities in a manner that benefits society as a whole, rather than just focusing solely on maximizing profits. It is about taking into consideration the impact of our actions on others and making efforts to contribute positively to the greater good. By promoting social responsibility, we can create a more sustainable and equitable world for present and future generations.

One of the key ways to promote social responsibility is through education and awareness. By educating individuals and organizations about the importance of social responsibility, we can increase their understanding of the impact of their actions and encourage them to make more ethical decisions. This can be done through workshops, training sessions, and public awareness campaigns that highlight the benefits of being socially responsible. By raising awareness about social responsibility, we can help create a culture that values ethical behavior and encourages individuals and organizations to act in a way that benefits society.

Another important way to promote social responsibility is through policy and regulation. Governments and regulatory bodies play a crucial role in shaping the behavior of individuals and organizations by creating laws and regulations that promote social responsibility. By implementing policies that require businesses to adhere to ethical standards and take into consideration the impact of their actions on society and the environment, we can create a more responsible and sustainable business environment. This can include regulations that require companies to disclose their environmental and social impact, as well as laws that encourage corporate social responsibility practices.

Corporate social responsibility (CSR) is another important aspect of promoting social responsibility. CSR refers to the voluntary actions that companies take to address social and environmental issues, beyond what is required by law. By engaging in CSR activities, companies can demonstrate their commitment to being good corporate citizens and contribute to the well-being of society. This can include initiatives such as donating to charity, supporting local communities, and implementing sustainable business practices. By promoting CSR, companies can build trust with their stakeholders and position themselves as leaders in corporate social responsibility.

Collaboration and partnerships are also key to promoting social responsibility. By working together with other organizations, government agencies, and NGOs, we can leverage our collective resources and expertise to address social and environmental issues more effectively. By collaborating with other like-minded partners, we can develop innovative solutions to complex problems, share best practices, and amplify our impact. By fostering collaboration and partnerships, we can create a more cohesive and coordinated approach to promoting social responsibility. By educating individuals and organizations, implementing policies and regulations, engaging in CSR activities, and fostering collaboration and partnerships, we can encourage a culture of social responsibility that benefits both society and the environment. By promoting social responsibility, we can create a better world for all and ensure a brighter future for generations to come.

Chapter 19: Celebrating Achievements and Milestones

- RECOGNIZING AND CELEBRATING successes

Recognizing and celebrating successes is a fundamental aspect of human behavior and motivation. When individuals achieve their goals and experience success, it is important to acknowledge their accomplishments and provide positive reinforcement. This recognition not only boosts the individual's self-esteem and confidence but also reinforces the behavior that led to the success. In a professional setting, recognizing and celebrating successes can improve morale, engagement, and productivity among employees. By recognizing and celebrating achievements, organizations can create a culture of appreciation and positivity that motivates individuals to strive for excellence.

One of the key benefits of recognizing and celebrating successes is the positive impact it has on an individual's motivation and performance. When individuals feel acknowledged and appreciated for their hard work and achievements, it serves as a powerful motivator to continue performing at a high level. Recognition can come in various forms, including verbal praise, awards, promotions, bonuses, or public acknowledgment. These gestures communicate to the individual that their efforts are valued and that their contributions have made a significant impact. This validation boosts their confidence and encourages them to continue working towards their goals with enthusiasm and dedication.

In addition to motivating individuals, recognizing and celebrating successes also fosters a sense of camaraderie and teamwork within an organization. When achievements are celebrated collectively, it reinforces the idea that success is a shared responsibility and that everyone plays a vital role in the organization's success. This sense of unity and collaboration can strengthen relationships among team members and create a positive work environment where individuals feel supported and appreciated. Celebrating successes together can also inspire others to emulate the behavior and strive for their own accomplishments, creating a culture of excellence and continuous improvement.

Moreover, recognizing and celebrating successes can have a ripple effect that extends beyond the individual or team being acknowledged. When achievements are publicized and celebrated, it sends a powerful message to the entire organization that hard work and dedication are valued and rewarded. This can motivate others to set ambitious goals, take on challenges, and push themselves to achieve greatness. By shining a spotlight on success stories, organizations can inspire others to reach their full potential and create a culture of high performance and achievement. Recognizing and celebrating successes can also attract and retain top talent, as individuals are more likely to thrive in an environment that appreciates and rewards their efforts.

It is important to note that recognizing and celebrating successes should be done in a genuine and authentic manner. Empty gestures or insincere praise can backfire and undermine the morale and motivation of individuals. Recognition should be personalized and tailored to the individual's preferences and style, taking into account their unique strengths and contributions. Celebrations should also be inclusive and accessible to all employees, regardless of their role or level within the organization. By creating a culture of recognition and celebration that is transparent and fair, organizations can reinforce positive behavior and motivate individuals to strive for excellence. By acknowledging and rewarding achievements, organizations can create a culture of appreciation and positivity that inspires individuals to strive for excellence. Celebrating successes collectively can foster a sense of unity and teamwork, while also motivating others to set ambitious goals and push themselves to achieve greatness. To create a culture of recognition and celebration, organizations should ensure that gestures are genuine, personalized, and inclusive, and that they communicate the value of hard work and dedication. By recognizing and celebrating successes, organizations can foster a culture of high performance and achievement that benefits both individuals and the organization as a whole.

- Setting and achieving goals

Setting and achieving goals is a fundamental aspect of success in both personal and professional endeavors. Goal setting provides individuals with a roadmap to follow, a clear direction to move towards, and a sense of purpose and motivation. However, merely setting goals is not enough; one must also work diligently towards achieving them. In this essay, we will explore the importance of setting goals, the process of setting effective goals, and strategies for achieving those goals.

First and foremost, setting goals gives individuals a sense of direction and purpose. Without clear goals, one may feel lost or unsure of where they are heading in life. Goals serve as a guiding light, helping individuals make decisions and prioritize their actions. They provide a sense of focus and motivation, ensuring that individuals stay on track and do not deviate from their desired path. Whether the goal is personal, professional, academic, or fitness-related, setting specific, measurable, achievable, relevant, and time-bound (SMART) goals is key to success.

In order to set effective goals, one must follow a systematic process. The first step is to identify the goal itself. What is it that you want to achieve. Be specific and clear about your goal, whether it's to lose weight, get a promotion at work, or run a marathon. Next, break down the goal into smaller, manageable steps. This will make the goal more achievable and help you stay motivated as you progress towards it. Set deadlines for each step to keep yourself accountable and on track. Additionally, consider any obstacles or challenges that may arise along the way and come up with strategies to overcome them. To bring to a close, regularly review and adjust your goals as needed to ensure that they remain relevant and aligned with your overall objectives.

Once you have set your goals, the next step is to work towards achieving them. This requires commitment, perseverance, and a positive attitude. It's important to stay focused and disciplined, even when faced with setbacks or obstacles. Stay motivated by reminding yourself of the benefits of achieving your goals and the positive impact it will have on your life. Surround yourself with supportive individuals who encourage and motivate you to keep going. Additionally, celebrate small victories along the way to boost your confidence and momentum. Remember that success is a journey, and achieving your goals is not always easy, but with dedication and hard work, anything is possible. By setting clear and specific goals, following a systematic process, and staying committed and motivated, individuals can accomplish their aspirations and lead fulfilling lives. Remember to be patient and persistent, as success rarely happens overnight. With the right mindset and determination, you can overcome any challenge and achieve even the most ambitious goals. So, set your goals, create a plan to achieve them, and get ready to transform your dreams into reality.

- Reflecting on growth and progress

Reflection is a powerful tool for personal and professional growth. It allows individuals to look back on their experiences, analyze their successes and failures, and use that knowledge to make informed decisions moving forward. In the context of progress, reflection is key to understanding how far we have come and what steps we need to take to continue growing.

When reflecting on growth and progress, it is important to first define what these concepts mean to you personally. Growth can take many forms - it can be intellectual, emotional, professional, or personal. Progress, on the other hand, typically refers to the tangible outcomes of our growth, such as achieving certain goals or reaching specific milestones. By taking the time to clearly outline what growth and progress mean to you, you can better assess your own development and identify areas for improvement.

One of the most effective ways to reflect on your growth and progress is to keep a journal. Writing down your thoughts, feelings, and experiences can help you gain clarity and insight into your own development. Try setting aside a few minutes each day to jot down your thoughts on how you are progressing towards your goals, what challenges you have faced, and what lessons you have learned along the way. By regularly reviewing your journal entries, you can track your growth over time and identify patterns that may be hindering your progress.

In addition to journaling, seeking feedback from others can also be a valuable tool for reflecting on growth and progress. Ask friends, family members, mentors, or colleagues for their honest assessment of your strengths, weaknesses, and areas for improvement. Hearing different perspectives can provide valuable insights and help you see blind spots that you may not have been aware of. Remember to approach feedback with an open mind and a willingness to learn and grow from it.

Another important aspect of reflecting on growth and progress is celebrating your successes. It is easy to get caught up in the daily grind and lose sight of how far you have come. Take the time to acknowledge your achievements, no matter how small they may seem. Celebrating your successes can boost your confidence, motivate you to keep pushing forward, and remind you of your abilities when faced with challenges.

It is also important to reflect on your setbacks and failures. While it may be tempting to sweep them under the rug and move on, taking the time to analyze what went wrong can provide valuable insights for future growth. Ask yourself what you could have done differently, what lessons you can learn from the experience, and how you can apply those lessons moving forward. Remember, setbacks are a natural part of the growth process, and it is how we respond to them that ultimately determines our progress. By taking the time to journal, seek feedback, celebrate successes, and learn from setbacks, you can gain valuable insights into your own growth journey and make informed decisions moving forward. Remember, growth is a continuous process, and progress is not always linear. Embrace the journey, stay open to feedback, and keep striving for personal and professional growth.

Chapter 20: Conclusion

....

- RECAP OF KEY POINTS

Recap of Key Points:

In this comprehensive discussion, we have explored a range of important concepts and ideas related to the topic at hand. To begin with, we delved into the central theme of the importance of communication in professional settings. We highlighted the significance of clear and effective communication in facilitating collaboration, resolving conflicts, and achieving organizational goals. We emphasized the need for active listening, empathy, and open-mindedness in fostering meaningful and productive communication exchanges.

Moreover, we examined the role of diversity and inclusivity in modern workplaces. We underscored the value of embracing diversity as a source of innovation, creativity, and enhanced decision-making. We discussed the importance of creating inclusive environments where all individuals feel respected, valued, and empowered to contribute their unique perspectives and talents. We also explored strategies for promoting diversity and inclusivity, such as mentoring programs, unconscious bias training, and diversity recruitment initiatives.

Furthermore, we explored the concept of emotional intelligence and its relevance to professional success. We defined emotional intelligence as the ability to recognize and manage one's own emotions, as well as understand and influence the emotions of others. We highlighted the impact of emotional intelligence on leadership effectiveness, team dynamics, and interpersonal relationships. We also discussed ways to enhance emotional intelligence, such as practicing self-awareness, empathy, and emotional regulation.

Additionally, we discussed the importance of growth mindset in fostering continuous learning and development. We defined growth mindset as the belief that abilities and intelligence can be developed through effort, perseverance, and learning from failure. We emphasized the role of growth mindset in promoting resilience, adaptability, and a willingness to take on new challenges.

We also explored strategies for cultivating a growth mindset, including seeking feedback, setting ambitious goals, and embracing a willingness to learn from mistakes. By embracing these principles and practices, individuals and organizations can cultivate a culture of collaboration, creativity, and continuous learning that is essential for success in today's dynamic and fast-paced work environments. We encourage readers to reflect on these key points and consider how they can apply these principles in their own professional lives to drive personal and organizational growth.

- Commitment to empowered parenting

Empowered parenting is a concept that emphasizes the importance of parents being actively engaged in their children's upbringing and development. It involves taking a proactive approach to parenting, where parents are committed to providing their children with the necessary tools, resources, and support to help them thrive and reach their full potential. Empowered parenting is not about being overbearing or controlling, but rather about being present, attentive, and guiding in a way that fosters independence and self-esteem.

One key aspect of empowered parenting is the commitment to building strong and healthy relationships with children. This involves being emotionally available, listening to their concerns, and respecting their autonomy. By creating a nurturing and supportive environment, parents can help children feel safe and secure, which is essential for their emotional well-being. Empowered parents also prioritize communication and open dialogue, encouraging their children to express their thoughts and feelings freely without fear of judgment or retribution.

Another important facet of empowered parenting is the emphasis on teaching children essential life skills. This includes everything from basic hygiene and nutrition to more complex skills such as problem-solving, decision-making, and conflict resolution. By instilling these skills early on, parents can help their children become capable and confident individuals who are equipped to navigate the challenges of adulthood. Empowered parents understand the importance of setting boundaries and providing structure, while also allowing room for exploration and growth.

Empowered parenting also involves fostering a sense of autonomy and independence in children. This means allowing them to make choices and decisions for themselves, while also providing guidance and support when needed. Empowered parents encourage their children to think for themselves and take responsibility for their actions, helping them develop a strong sense of self-worth and confidence. By nurturing autonomy, parents can help children develop a sense of agency and empowerment that will serve them well throughout their lives.

Furthermore, empowered parenting is rooted in a commitment to lifelong learning and personal growth. Parents who are committed to empowered parenting understand that they are not perfect and that they too can benefit from self-reflection and self-improvement. By modeling a growth mindset and a willingness to learn from their mistakes, parents can show their children the importance of resilience, perseverance, and humility. This creates a culture of continuous learning and improvement within the family that benefits everyone involved. Empowered parents understand that parenting is a dynamic and ever-evolving process that requires patience, empathy, and a genuine desire to see their children succeed. By actively engaging in their children's lives and providing them with the support and guidance they need, empowered parents can help raise confident, capable, and resilient individuals who are prepared to face the challenges of the future.

- Looking ahead to the future of raising great kids

As parents, caregivers, and educators, looking ahead to the future of raising great kids is a crucial task. In today's fast-paced and ever-changing world, it is essential to prepare our children for the challenges and opportunities that lie ahead. Raising great kids goes beyond just ensuring they excel academically; it involves nurturing their social, emotional, and cognitive development to help them become well-rounded individuals who can thrive in the future.

One of the key aspects of raising great kids is fostering a positive and nurturing environment at home. Children thrive when they feel loved, supported, and valued by their parents and caregivers. Spending quality time with your child, engaging in meaningful conversations, and actively listening to their thoughts and feelings can help build a strong bond and instill a sense of security and trust. Additionally, setting clear boundaries, providing structure and routine, and enforcing consistent discipline can help children feel safe and secure, leading to a healthy and stable upbringing.

In addition to the home environment, education plays a crucial role in raising great kids. As parents and educators, it is essential to provide children with a well-rounded education that goes beyond academics. Teaching kids valuable life skills such as problem-solving, critical thinking, communication, and collaboration can help them navigate the complexities of the future with confidence and resilience. Moreover, promoting a love for learning, encouraging curiosity, and fostering a growth mindset can empower children to embrace challenges, learn from failures, and strive for continuous improvement.

Another important aspect of raising great kids is promoting social and emotional development. In today's digital age, children are exposed to various forms of social media, online gaming, and virtual communication, which can impact their social and emotional well-being. It is crucial for parents and caregivers to monitor and guide their children's online activities, promote healthy relationships, and encourage face-to-face interactions. Teaching kids empathy, compassion, and conflict resolution skills can help them develop strong interpersonal relationships and navigate social situations effectively.

Looking ahead to the future, it is important to prepare children for the globalized and interconnected world they will inherit. Teaching kids about cultural diversity, global citizenship, and environmental sustainability can help instill a sense of empathy, respect, and responsibility towards others and the planet. Encouraging children to explore different cultures, learn new languages, and engage in community service can broaden their perspectives and foster a sense of social responsibility and civic engagement. By prioritizing the physical, emotional, social, and cognitive well-being of our children, we can help them develop the skills, values, and attitudes needed to thrive in the rapidly changing world. As parents, caregivers, and educators, it is our responsibility to foster the potential of every child and empower them to become compassionate, resilient, and successful individuals who can make a positive impact on the world.